PARANORMAL
SUSSEX

PARANORMAL SUSSEX

DAVID SCANLAN

AMBERLEY

First published 2009

Amberley Publishing
Cirencester Road, Chalford,
Stroud, Gloucestershire, GL6 8PE

www.amberley-books.com

British Library Cataloguing in Publication Data.
A catalogue record for this book is available from the British Library.

ISBN 978 1 84868 462 1

Typesetting and origination by Amberley Publishing
Printed in Great Britain

CONTENTS

LIST OF ILLUSTRATIONS 7

ACKNOWLEDGEMENTS 9

FOREWORD 11

INTRODUCTION 13
    How to use this book 13

A GAZETTEER OF SUSSEX HAUNTINGS
    A23, Between Brighton and Pyecombe, East & West Sussex 15
    Amberley Castle Hotel, near Arundel, West Sussex 15
    Anne of Cleves House, Lewes, East Sussex 16
    Arundel Castle, Arundel, West Sussex 19
    Arundel Cathedral, Arundel, West Sussex 21
    Arundel Gaol, Arundel, West Sussex 21
    Bateman's, Burwash, East Sussex 23
    Battle Abbey, Battle, East Sussex 23
    Beachy Head, Eastbourne, East Sussex 29
    Bexhill Police Station, Bexhill, East Sussex 29
    Bramber Castle, Bramber, West Sussex 29
    Brede Place, Brede, East Sussex 30
    Chanctonbury Ring, West Sussex 30
    Cissbury Ring, Worthing, West Sussex 33
    Clapham Woods, Clapham, West Sussex 33
    Coach and Horses, St Pancras, Chichester, West Sussex 36
    Comet Store, Worthing, West Sussex 37
    Connaught Theatre, Worthing, West Sussex 38
    Cowdray House, Midhurst, West Sussex 39
    Cuckfield Park, Cuckfield, West Sussex 43
    Deans Place Hotel, Alfriston, East Sussex 45
    Devonshire Park Theatre, Eastbourne, East Sussex 45
    Fisherman's Joy, East Street, Selsey, West Sussex 46
    Ford Airfield, Ford, West Sussex 49
    Foredown Tower, Portslade, East Sussex 49

Glydwish Woods, nr Burwash, East Sussex   51
Goodwood House, Chichester, West Sussex   51
Hayes Hotel, Northiam, East Sussex   55
Herstmonceux Castle, Hailsham, East Sussex   56
HM Prison Lewes, Lewes, East Sussex   57
Holy Trinity Church, Bosham, West Sussex   58
Iron Duke Hotel, Hove, East Sussex   58
King and Queen Public House, Brighton, East Sussex   59
Kingley Vale, Stoughton, West Sussex   61
Kings Head Public House, Cuckfield, West Sussex   61
Kneep Castle, West Grinstead, West Sussex   62
Lion Hotel, Nyetimber, West Sussex   62
Meeting House, Meeting House Lane, Brighton, East Sussex   63
Mermaid Inn, Rye, East Sussex   63
Michelham Priory, Upper Dicker, East Sussex   64
Mint House, Pevensey, East Sussex   67
Mothercare Shop, Chichester, West Sussex   68
Nan Tucks Lane, Buxted, East Sussex   68
Old Police Cells Museum, Brighton Town Hall, Brighton, East Sussex   69
Pashley Manor, Ticehurst, East Sussex   70
Pevensey Castle, Pevensey, East Sussex   70
Pevensey Courthouse, Pevensey, East Sussex   72
Preston Manor, Brighton, East Sussex   74
Queens Head, Icklesham, Winchelsea, East Sussex   76
Racton Ruin, nr Funtington, West Sussex   77
Royal Hippodrome, Eastbourne, East Sussex   78
Saint Mary the Virgin Church, Westham, Pevensey, East Sussex   79
Saint Nicholas' Church, Arundel, West Sussex   80
Sea Life Centre, Brighton, East Sussex   80
Seven Stars, Robertsbridge, East Sussex   81
The Wingrove Inn, Alfriston, East Sussex   82
Verdley Castle, near Midhurst, West Sussex   83
Ye Olde Smugglers Inn, Alfriston, East Sussex   83

GHOST HUNTING – AN INTRODUCTION   85

GET INVOLVED   89

BIBLIOGRAPHY   91

ABOUT THE AUTHOR   93

LIST OF ILLUSTRATIONS

Anne of Cleves House in Lewes, East Sussex   17
The Knights' Table at Anne of Cleves House   18
The impressive and dominating façade of Arundel Castle   19
Arundel Town Hall   22
Senlac Hill   24
A section of the Bayeux tapestry.   25
The monument marking where King Harold was killed   26
The main gatehouse of Battle Abbey   27
The undercroft of Battle Abbey   28
The ring of trees planted at the summit of Chanctonbury Hill   31
An occult pentagram found in Clapham woods   34
The Sacred Beech Tree, also known as the Altar Tree   35
Cowdray House, near Midhurst   40
The ruins of Cowdray House   41
The beautiful house that is Cuckfield Park   43
The gateway to Cuckfield Park   44
The Devonshire Park Theatre, Eastbourne.   46
The Fisherman's Joy Public House in East Street, Selsey   47
The main corridor of the Fisherman's Joy Public House   48
Foredown Tower in Portslade   50
Herstmonceux Castle   57
The King and Queen Public House in Brighton   60
Michelham Priory   65
The prior's room at Michelham Priory   66
The remains of the Roman castle at Pevensey   71
The Pevensey Courthouse in East Sussex   73
The drawing room of Preston Manor, Brighton   75
The remains of the curious, and haunted, ruin that is Racton   77
The Royal Hippodrome Theatre in Eastbourne   79
An example of some of the author's paranormal investigation equipment   87
The author outside a haunted church   93

ACKNOWLEDGEMENTS

Susan Butcher and Samantha Clark of the *Sussex Express Newspaper*, Mel Butcher, Stuart Logan, Clifford Nicholson of the Ye Olde Smugglers Inn, Adrien Joly of Brighton and Hove City Council, who was of great help with the stories regarding Preston Manor, Paula Wrightson, Peter Lindars of the Iron Duke Hotel, Rosemary Nicolaou of English Heritage, Clint Symonds and Sussex Paranormal Research Group, Rosie Gray, Tim Brown of the Paranormal Investigation Group Sussex, Emma O'Connor of Sussex Past, Arron Weedall and West Sussex Paranormal Investigations, Brian Lambert, Pevensey Town Trust, Pevensey Courthouse, Jan Cox, British Paranormal Association, and my final thanks go to my good friend and fellow ghost hunter Bob Hunt who proofread *Paranormal Sussex*, wrote a kind foreword and made many useful suggestions.

FOREWORD

Welcome to author David Scanlan's third book on the paranormal. Like his first two books, *Paranormal Wiltshire* and *Paranormal Hampshire*, this book is well written, easy to read and thoroughly researched.

I work closely with David through his paranormal investigation group, the Hampshire Ghost Club (www.hampshireghostclub.net), I know his research methods well: the way all events are recorded, all possibilities examined before a paranormal explanation is even thought of, with clear concise reports available at the end of each investigation. This same work methodology has been brought to his books for the benefit of the reader; I know many stories were left out once they had been researched as the stories themselves proved to have very little basis in truth or at the very least were extremely exaggerated. After all what's the point of retelling old tales and keeping the belief that there are truths in some of these stories when there are not? It is time better spent to investigate true hauntings than to waste time investigating cases that are probably greatly erroneous. David has attempted to keep only the plausible stories within the leaves of his books and *Paranormal Sussex* excels at this.

As with the first two books, you will find this one well laid out, and full of interesting information with the right combination of historical facts and paranormal events. The stories will be from many places you can visit for yourself, both in the daytime and even at night if you fancy a spot of your own ghost hunting, and who knows, maybe you will be the one that is lucky enough to be able to confirm the sightings of the ghosts described here.

If you do want to get involved in investigating ghosts and hauntings then be sure to check out the back of *Paranormal Sussex* for a basic guide on ghost hunting and ghost hunting equipment and also for a selected list of the most respected Sussex-based paranormal investigation groups that would be happy to have you join them in their search for the dead!

Bob Hunt
Team Leader and Investigator of The Hampshire Ghost Club

INTRODUCTION

No visitor to the historical county of Sussex can remain unimpressed when they encounter the history and legends of his stunning county. With its impressive scenery, sprawling cities, quiet idyllic villages and its bustling towns, Sussex has something to offer everyone.

Sussex has its fair share of fables and legends, as does any other county in the United Kingdom, but its ghost stories come into a realm of their own; what's more, the people of Sussex appear to be proud of their ghosts and throughout the writing of this book I have encountered and chatted merrily to many a person who has been happy to relay their take on many of the ghost stories of the county that have now become deeply imbedded into the cultural history of the place.

Sussex has been one of the most difficult counties for which to formulate, compile and write the stories and legends as there is so much conflicting information. One person will tell you one thing and another person will tell you another, and this obviously leaves one wondering which story is the truth. Have some of the older ghosts faded away or been forgotten, or have they simply been replaced with more up-to-date myths and legends? What cannot be disputed about Sussex is that people have experienced the weird and wonderful here.

Throughout my journey I have met many a wonderful person and paranormal investigation group and, although I have tried to include as many haunted places as possible within the confines of the book, many readers will inevitably notice stories that are not included. This is simply because of space limitations or the simple explanation is that a more in-depth knowledge of the haunting in question is so sparse in its facts and evidence that relaying an accurate story has not been possible. If I have failed to include any stories in here that you, the reader, deem essential then please do contact me via the publishers so that future editions and updates can be amended.

HOW TO USE THIS BOOK

As with my previous books, *Paranormal Hampshire* and *Paranormal Wiltshire* (both of which are available from Amberley Publishing), the format that worked best for *Paranormal Sussex* was to follow the simple, easy to understand, A-Z content for the book. This allows you to pick up and put down the book at will and also allows any reader, even a casual one, the ability to immediately research individual areas or locations.

As Sussex is split into two, West Sussex and East Sussex, I initially thought of dividing the stories and legends that I retell in this book into two seperate sections, but decided to join them as one in order to aid in the pleasure of reading this book. I hope this decision will in no way hinder your enjoyment of *Paranormal Sussex*. I have attempted to relay the stories told to me as accurately as possible, omitted stories that are blatantly fabricated and put right those stories which were thought to be paranormal for many years but have since been found to have rational explanations. I hope I have achieved what I set out to do with this book and that you relish delving into the mysteries, legends and lore of the county of Sussex.

A Gazetteer of Sussex Hauntings

A23, BETWEEN BRIGHTON AND PYECOMBE, EAST & WEST SUSSEX

The A23 is a road that is still fresh in the memories of many Sussex residents for it was the site, in 2004, of a horrific crash that claimed the lives of eight people, including that of a very young child.

The road has seen many accidents in its time. From people being struck whilst riding their bicycles to peoples' lives being taken away from them in car accidents, it is perhaps because of the dangers of this road, past and present, that people claim it is haunted.

Sightings of phantom shapes flitting across the road and vanishing have been reported here since the 1960s. Witnesses to these road ghosts, phantom hitch-hikers, call them what you will, claim to have seen an indistinct masculine shape on the A23 near to Handcross Hill, and towards the small village of Pyecombe, some seven or so miles north of Brighton, the sightings increase.

The ghost of a man wearing a short sleeved shirt, the spectre of a blonde woman wearing what appears to be a mackintosh type of coat, and the phantom of a blonde girl, who appears to be limping and could very well be linked to a motorbike accident in the area, have all been seen in the vicinity.

If you happen to be travelling the A23 sometime in the future then please do promise me two things. One, that you take great care whilst travelling this notorious road, and two, please do let me know if you encounter any of the aforementioned ghosts!

AMBERLEY CASTLE HOTEL, NEAR ARUNDEL, WEST SUSSEX

A mere five miles away from the popular tourist-destination town of Arundel lies the small parish of Amberley. The village is known today for its very popular working museum that details the industrial heritage of the area and surrounding districts and makes for a very entertaining and educational experience.

A lesser known venue in the village is Amberley Castle, which is today a very high-class hotel sporting nineteen luxury rooms and a whole assortment of recreational facilities including a golf course, croquet lawn, tennis courts, oh, and not forgetting of course . . . a resident ghost!

The hotel boasts a history than spans over 900 years and was originally constructed as a place of protection for the clergy. The castle has had some impressive visitors over the years including Queens Elizabeth I and II, Kings Henry V, VII and VIII, Queen Victoria, King George V and many more. The sheer history that any visitor can absorb whilst spending time within the hotel's hallowed walls is more than enough, but throw a classic ghost story on top and what more could you possibly want?

The local story surrounding the ghost that haunts here is that a former maid was abused by one of the bishops who lived at the castle; some sources claim the girl was actually involved in a relationship with the bishop but we shall unfortunately never know the full story as history has a knack of covering these little facts up and burying them almost completely. Unable to deal with the shame of her abuse she decided to take her own life by throwing herself off the sixty-foot-high curtain wall to her certain death. For as many theories that are put forward to explain the sightings of the sad looking ghost of the girl just as many are put forward to explain the young lady's death, and whilst researching this book I have come across numerous suggestions that the girl actually died in childbirth, by contracting malaria or even marsh fever.

Although we cannot say for certain what happened in this young lady's life, or her death for that matter, the fact cannot be taken away that perfectly normal and sane people have reported seeing the ghost of a young girl, whom many say is accompanied by a sense of sadness and despair, in the area of the palace's former kitchens.

ANNE OF CLEVES HOUSE, LEWES, EAST SUSSEX

A little to the south of the main town centre of Lewes lies Anne of Cleves House, a house that was given to the former wife of Henry VIII as part of her divorce settlement in 1541.

For many years there has been an intriguing legend concerning a large table, known as the Knights' Table, which is made from Sussex marble and dates from the medieval period. The table originally came from a house at South Malling and it was at this house that the knights who had slain Thomas à Becket, the Archbishop of Canterbury, in 1170 rested after doing their dirty deed.

It's claimed that when the knights, Reginald Fitzurse, Hugh de Moreville, William de Tracey and Richard le Bret, threw their gauntlets and swords onto

Anne of Cleves House in Lewes, East Sussex. The house was part of a divorce settlement to one of Henry VIII's wives and is now home to a legendary table and two female spectres, although their presence is unconfirmed to date! Photo © Sussex Archaeological Society

the table, the table promptly threw the knights' gauntlets and swords to the floor, and no matter how much persuasion was applied, the table would not allow the knights' murderous items to rest upon its surface. The extraordinary myth, and I refer to it as a myth for good reason, is that the table is meant to rotate wildly and speak the words 'Remember poor Thomas' on 29 December every year, or, according to the 1994 book by John Brooks entitled *The Good Ghost Guide*, it does!

Unfortunately, the story is nothing more than a myth, as I discovered when I spoke to Emma O'Connor who is the current curator at Anne of Cleves House. When I asked Emma about the legend of the table spinning wildly every 29 December she erupted in laughter and said 'I've heard it all now. I know of the story of the knights placing their gauntlets and swords on the table and their garb being thrown to the floor but the table spinning round and speaking every 29 December is absolutely ridiculous. There is no possibility of it happening. The table is three or four inches thick and is a considerable weight.'

The Knights' Table at Anne of Cleves House. Legend tells us that the men who cruelly slaughtered St Thomas à Becket threw their gauntlets and weapons onto the table, the table then promptly threw them off again! Photo © Sussex Archaeological Society

Perhaps the table did throw the knights' equipment to the floor many centuries ago, could it be that this was perceived as an omen by the people at the house and that's how the story has come to survive to this day? Or could it be, considering the table's weight, that the table was unstable in the first place and that the knights' apparel just took a perfectly logical tumble? Whatever the truth, it is certain that this story has become embellished and built upon over the centuries.

What about other ghosts at Anne of Cleves House? There are stories of the ghost of an old lady and that of a woman hanging by a rope from one of the roof beams. 'I have been curator here for about eighteen years now and I have never heard either of those stories. We get people saying they feel cold spots but that's something perfectly natural in a house of this age. We are hopefully going to be letting ghost hunters into the house soon so hopefully they might be able to shed some light onto the mysteries of Anne of Cleves House in the not-too-distant future.'

The impressive and dominating façade of Arundel Castle, home to four ghostly occupants, including an omen of impending death.

ARUNDEL CASTLE, ARUNDEL, WEST SUSSEX

As the visitor, or even the passer-by, entering the small market town of Arundel in West Sussex, you immediately notice two auspicious landmarks that overlook the small town.

Approaching from the west your gaze is immediately drawn to the grand Arundel cathedral, and continuing a short way on you are taken aback by the view of Arundel Castle. The castle has been the ancestral seat of the Dukes of Norfolk for many centuries, although its construction and history stems from much further back in the eleventh century. The castle looks very new in its appearance and this is due to the major restoration work undertaken by Charles Howard (1746-1815), the 11th Duke of Norfolk and in particular by Henry Howard (1847-1917), 15th Duke of Norfolk.

Having such a rich tapestry of history one would expect to find a whole assortment of ghosts here, but surprisingly there are no ghosts of kings, queens, lords or ladies, but the restless wraiths of average, everyday folk and even an animal.

Possibly the most famous of Arundel Castle's ghosts is that of a kitchen boy. Many years back the young lad worked in the kitchens of the castle and it's alleged that his superior was not very kind in his treatment of the boy: his abuse pushing the child into an early grave. There have been reports of people hearing the banging and crashing of pots and pans as the juvenile kitchen assistant furiously cleans the never-ending piles of dirty cooking utensils.

One of the most astounding rooms in the castle is the library. As soon as you enter here you are instantly aware of the hush that descends around the room; you can't help but get swept up in the silence and remain silent as you examine the rows and rows of books, artwork and precious items that surround you. Perhaps it is this tranquillity that binds our second ghost to this room. The apparition, of what has been described as a royalist cavalier, has been witnessed looking through the library's collection of books. The first sighting of this apparition heralds from the early seventeenth century, which has led many people to theorise that this ghost originates from the time of King Charles I (1600-1649), although there is no conclusive proof of this and the ghost could actually be much older, or younger for that matter, than is estimated. Not being able to even place this ghost from a specific period leads to severe problems in understanding who he is or why he haunts the castle.

Next we come to Hiorne Tower. This unusual structure was built by Charles Howard, 11th Duke of Norfolk. When the Duke was planning his restoration of Arundel Castle he decided to put to the test the designs of the architect, Francis Hiorne, who was desperately looking to be commissioned to undertake the work. Although the tower was completed, Francis died shortly after and never got the chance to have his dream fulfilled. Perhaps it is the tower's association with its designer's tragic demise and disappointment that drew a young lady here who took her own life. In true ghost story fashion, the lady had a love affair that didn't quite work out the way she wanted it to and, deciding that there was nothing more that could be done, she climbed the steep hill that the tower stands on, ascended the stairs and then threw herself from the top, plummeting to her death. The ghostly suicide has been witnessed time and again since the harrowing act took place.

Ornithophobia is described as 'the irrational fear or phobia of birds'. Some readers of *Paranormal Sussex* will be thinking 'What? How can you be scared of birds?' Well, if you happen to come across the phantom white bird that flaps at the windows of Arundel Castle you would well understand the family's reluctance to see this feathered friend, for it is meant to be seen by a member of the household and it is treated as an omen of a forthcoming death in the family, usually the head of the family line! Not a sighting to be taken lightly at all.

ARUNDEL CATHEDRAL, ARUNDEL, WEST SUSSEX

Perched on a hill overlooking Arundel town is Arundel Cathedral, built in 1873 and dedicated to Our Lady and St Phillip in 1965. St Phillip was the 20th Earl of Arundel and one of the forty Catholic martyrs of England and Wales. He was imprisoned in the Tower of London in 1585 on trumped up charges of treason against Queen Elizabeth I. The Earl eventually died in the Tower of London of dysentery on 15 October 1595. His mortal remains were moved into the cathedral from the Fitzalan Chapel in 1971.

With such a strong religious conviction, an awful death and the prestige of having a cathedral dedicated to your memory, one would think that the ghost that haunts here would be the spirit of St Phillip himself, but alas it is not. It is, however, the spirit of another humble and religious character.

Reverend John Butt, also know as Bishop Butt as he formally held the title of Bishop of Southwark until his resignation in 1897, used the cathedral for his retirement and it appears that although the reverend only spent a short time at the cathedral he has become entwined in its very fabric. His ghost has been seen sitting in his old room near to the presbytery and also on the staircase.

ARUNDEL GAOL, ARUNDEL, WEST SUSSEX

Even though I herald from Hampshire, Arundel Gaol has a special place in my heart. I happened to stumble across the old gaol back in April 2005. As I went on a tour of the place, learning about its history, I managed to grab the attention of the manager and asked if he had any unusual experiences at the gaol that he couldn't explain.

After the tour had finished the manager went on to tell me of his feelings of being watched and sensing that you 'were never alone'. Regaling him with stories of my own experiences and those of the Hampshire Ghost Club, we were duly invited to come along to the gaol one night and conduct an investigation here and see if we could gather any evidence of any unusual, possibly supernatural, phenomena.

Apart from being aware of the manager's feeling of being watched whilst alone in the place we went in totally blind, not knowing if the place was definitely haunted or not, which may seem unusual for a paranormal investigation group to do, but it has paid off in the past.

Arundel Town Hall. Below the town hall lies Arundel Gaol where paranormal enthusiasts have started to discover a plethora of supernatural happenings.

During our investigation at Arundel Gaol we noted various unusual occurrences including the supernatural voice of a female child saying 'He's coming' that was captured on a dictaphone, unexpected variations in the electromagnetic background, sensations of being touched, and an unusual feeling that one cell in particular felt like 'it was pulsing', as was reported by investigators Scott Pritchard and Sharon Thornton.

The most unusual experience that happened during the investigation was when investigator Scott Pritchard suddenly felt he was being pushed to the floor by unseen hands. I have no doubt that more of the gaol's secrets will be revealed to us in time, more so now than ever as paranormal investigation groups descend upon the gaol in their droves.

BATEMAN'S, BURWASH, EAST SUSSEX

Bateman's is currently in the possession of the National Trust and was formerly the home to one the county's most famous residents, Rudyard Kipling. Kipling was a renowned writer and poet and is remembered for his memorable works such as the *Just So Stories, Kim* and of course, many a child's favourite, *The Jungle Book.*

Kipling purchased Bateman's mansion and grounds in 1902 for the princely sum of £9,300. The house itself dates back to at least 1634. Obviously with a house this age Kipling was not the only occupant, but it seems that the ghosts that haunt here originate not from a long-gone era but from the time of Kipling himself.

People claim to have witnessed the ghost of Rudyard Kipling himself, standing at his desk in his study which has been left in situ from the time Kipling left this mortal world. The ghost of his wife has also been reported, tending the flowerbeds outside Kipling's study window.

I had the opportunity of speaking to the current visitor services manager at Bateman's, Fiona Hancock, who told me 'I know that when the Kiplings lived here they had a maid who claimed to be able to sense a presence in one of the rooms and there is also the tale that the daughter of one of the former millers threw herself from the mill in a classic love story type of legend. The death of the miller's daughter, though, is a rather classic romantic gesture and I think it could just be a myth; the story just doesn't add up. The ghost of the lady is allegedly seen leaping to her death from the mill'.

I asked Fiona if any paranormal encounters or experiences had been reported in recent years and was told 'No. Neither myself nor any of the staff working at Bateman's have ever had an encounter or seen anything untoward here.' Perhaps the ghosts of Kipling, his wife and the phantom miller's daughter have all moved onto pastures new?

BATTLE ABBEY, BATTLE, EAST SUSSEX

14 October 1066. It's a date we all learn about during our years at school and so it should be, for the entire course of English history changed on this date at a place called Senlac Hill.

On 4 January 1066 Edward the Confessor (1003-1066), the reigning King of England, left this mortal world and in doing so created a problem for two notable people of the time. Upon Edward's death, a distant cousin of the King, William, Duke of Normandy (1027-1087), came forward and claimed that the throne of England had been promised to him before the Confessor's death. However, Harold Godwinson (1022-1066) also claimed the King had named him as his

Senlac Hill. The site of the Battle of Hastings and the place where the entire course of English history changed in a single day. Photo © Kathy Gearing of The Ghost Club

successor before he died. Harold Godwinson was crowned King of England on 6 January 1066.

Furious at his loss of the English throne, William gathered together an invasion fleet and set forth for the shores of merry old England, arriving at Pevensey on 28 September 1066. From here, after establishing a castle, they moved further until they were met by King Harold and his followers at Senlac Hill where a battle would commence that is commonly known to many people around the world as the Battle of Hastings.

After the battle, which saw victory for William, the Duke erected an abbey commemorating his win over the English. The high altar of the abbey was built

A section of the Bayeux tapestry, which was woven as a record of the Norman conquest, which shows King Harold standing on the field of battle with an arrow protruding from his eye.

upon the spot where King Harold had died after being shot by an arrow in the eye, and then being hacked to death by members of the Norman cavalry.

But it is not to the leaves of this book that we turn for a history lesson – heaven knows there are numerous publications covering these events – but for the ghosts and supernatural legends surrounding the story of the eventual Battle of Hastings. Legends obviously abound here, as you would expect for a place that is so significant to English history, and there are plenty of stories concerning the ghosts of the long dead soldiers that lost their lives here.

The ghost of King Harold, wandering around covered in blood, has been reported, as has the spectral appearance of cavalry soldiers riding across the field of battle, both apparitions appearing on 14 October, the anniversary of the battle. A fountain of blood has allegedly been witnessed pouring out from the site of the high altar, the grass upon which the battle took place has been said to sweat blood, the ghost of the Duke's minstrel has been seen leading a phantom charge and children over the years have claimed to see a ghost of a man wearing an eyepatch looking out from one of the windows in

25

The high altar once stood where this monument now stands. This is the area where King Harold was killed and it's claimed that the altar once poured forth a fountain of mysterious blood. Photo © Kathy Gearing of The Ghost Club

the gatehouse. 'People have often claimed to have heard the sounds of battle,' said Rosemary Nicolaou, a current English Heritage employee based at Battle Abbey. 'I have had a few unusual experiences whilst working here but I think most things can be explained away quite easily, like the sounds of battle. We are quite close to the main town centre and people passing by, especially when the pubs are closing, do sound quite raucous at times so it's easy to see how these sounds could very well be mistaken for something all together more paranormal.'

Well, if rational thinking and a logical approach to the paranormal reports are applied does this mean that the ghosts that have been sighted here are nothing more than myth? Apparently not. Ms Nicolaou went on to tell me of a series of

The main gatehouse of Battle Abbey. The window in the uppermost centre of the gatehouse is where many people say that they have seen the ghost of a man wearing an eyepatch! Could this be the ghost of King Harold, another poor unfortunate soul or perhaps a trick of the light caused by the lead work in the windows? Photo © Kathy Gearing of The Ghost Club

events that do not seem to have a rational explanation no matter how logically you examine the experiences. Most of the unusual events these days appear to centre on the area of the undercroft of the abbey. 'We had a school group in here a few months ago and the teacher came up to me afterwards and asked why we had not told them that re-enactors were working that day. I told her that we didn't have any re-enactors working that day and she looked somewhat shocked for the children in her party had told her they wanted to talk to the man dressed up as a monk wearing a white robe with a red belt.

'A while ago we had a member of the public submit a photo to us showing an apparition hanging from an area where the old hanging post used to stand. I must admit though, I am not altogether convinced by this photo. I also heard the story

The undercroft of Battle Abbey has been the epicentre of a whole host of supernatural happenings including the sighting of ghostly monks and even a most unusual and surprising invasion of rotten apples! Photo © Kathy Gearing of The Ghost Club

that an electrician was working behind one of the displays in the museum and he turned around and witnessed the ghost of a monk looking directly at him and watching what the electrician was doing.

'The last thing which really did baffle me, but I don't know if it was paranormal or not, was the appearance of a lot of rotten apples in the undercroft. The undercroft was an area which in monastic times was used as a storage area for all kinds of things including fruit and vegetables. One winter, which had been particularly long, cold and wet, I went into one of the rooms and was greeted by this mass of rotten apples that were scattered all over the floor. I have no idea where they came from; I thought that was a little odd.'

BEACHY HEAD, EASTBOURNE, EAST SUSSEX

Despite the 100-million-year-old and 530-foot-high beauty of the cliffs at Beachy Head, they are better known as being a suicide hotspot for many people over the years, the most recent being in June 2009 when Neil and Kazumi Puttick leapt to their deaths following the tragic death of their five-year-old son.

Suicides are not a new thing at the cliffs for people have jumped to their demise possibly for centuries here, and perhaps the phantom of a black-clad monk who is meant to beckon people over the edge may well have something to do with some of the deaths that have occurred here. Legend states that the monk was shackled and thrown from the cliffs by Henry VIII's officials during the dissolution of the monasteries, although this has never been, and probably cannot be, confirmed as historical fact.

There have been reports of a ghostly woman walking the cliff edge before vanishing from sight and also a story concerning a lady who has been seen walking towards the edge of the cliff, clutching a baby in her arms, before disappearing over the precipice to certain death!

BEXHILL POLICE STATION, BEXHILL, EAST SUSSEX

There are reports of a phantom gentleman dressed in the clothing of the Edwardian era haunting this police station. Who he is and why he chooses to haunt such a place remains a mystery. When contacted in order to discuss this haunting, Sussex police could not throw any more light onto the topic.

BRAMBER CASTLE, BRAMBER, WEST SUSSEX

Bramber Castle is a motte-and-bailey-style fortification constructed by William de Braose, also spelt as Breose, around 1070. The de Braose clan thrived at Bramber for 133 years until the family incurred the wrath of King John in 1203. King John was becoming more and more alarmed at the outspokenness of his nobles and, unsure where the de Braose loyalties lay, the King requested that the children of William, the head of the family, be left in the custody of the King.

Being the caring parents these people obviously were, coupled with the fact that King John was not a man to be trusted in the slightest, the family fled to Ireland. Although thinking their safety was assured, they were quickly apprehended by the King's Men and returned to England. William de Braose, his wife and their children were all locked into a room at Windsor Castle and left to starve to death.

The remains of Bramber Castle are where the sorrowful wraiths of the de Braose children have been seen, emaciated and dressed in rags.

BREDE PLACE, BREDE, EAST SUSSEX

This fourteenth-century manor house, hidden away in the Sussex countryside, is the home to the ghost of a friendly vicar known as Father John, the ghost of a sixteenth-century maidservant who was hanged for stealing, and the ghost of a woman sporting Elizabethan costume. The most unusual ghost, or at least the one that is proposed as an explanation for one of the phenomena experienced in the house, is known as the Giant of Brede.

Sir Goddard Oxenbridge, a sixteenth-century owner of the house, who it has been claimed is the giant, is allegedly responsible for the sound of phantom footfalls on the house's staircase. Legend would lead us to believe that he was a terrible man that could not be killed by normal weapons, this supernatural power coming from his diet of young children. However, consider the usefulness of such a story for keeping people away from Brede Place when you're storing contraband goods . . . as did the smugglers who used the house in the eighteenth century. Perhaps Sir Goddard does indeed haunt Brede but the legends associated with this God-fearing man are completely wrong and unjust. It feels good to dismiss an undue reputation!

CHANCTONBURY RING, WEST SUSSEX

The South Downs is a place of immense mystery and myth and one of my particular favourite haunted sites, nestled on a ridgeway of the South Downs Way, is a place known today as Chanctonbury Ring.

Today the site stands out against the backdrop scenery because of a ring of trees that sits upon the hill's summit, but Chanctonbury Ring has been used by mankind since time immemorial. One of the most easily identifiable historical uses of the hill here is that of an Iron Age hill fort that was in use from around the sixth century BC. Archaeological excavations here, albeit somewhat minimal as the site has never been fully excavated, revealed that the hill had been used since a much earlier time as remains of flint work from the Neolithic, New Stone Age, period of history has been discovered here.

The hill was obviously important to our forefathers as a defensive home but when the Romans came to the area they also recognised the importance of the ring and established, over a period of time, two separate temples on the site. Already we can see that three separate peoples from history were drawn to the ring for its uses: the Neolithic people, Iron Age Celts and, of course, the Romans.

The ring of trees that were planted at the summit of Chanctonbury Hill gave the place its name. It's also the home to some frightening experiences including people being attacked by invisible forces and witnesses of mysterious lights in the sky that some have suggested are alien spacecraft. Photo © Stuart Logan

It is probably because of its importance to the local area that so many strange and unusual stories about the ring have now become embroiled in local legend. Women looking to conceive a child are encouraged to sleep under the trees in order to increase their fertility; reciting Shakespeare's *A Midsummer Night's Dream* at the time of the Summer Solstice allegedly encourages the appearance of little people who then proceed to run around you; walk or run around the ring twelve times at midnight on mid-summer's eve and you will be approached by the ghost of a long-dead druid. But the most extraordinary tale tells that the ring was actually created by the Devil and it is said that if you walk around the ring anti-clockwise seven times the Devil will appear before you and offer you a bowl of soup, some legends claim it is milk. Very kind gesture you may well think until he asks for your soul in return . . . you have been warned!

With so many unusual and spooky tales surrounding the ring it is hardly surprising to learn that people have encountered the weird and wonderful here. Paranormal and Occult researcher Stuart Logan told me about some of the past reported events that have still defied rational explanation. 'In 1967 some university students decided to camp out at the ring overnight to take tape recordings and photographs of any strange activity that may have occurred there. It is reported that they became "panic-stricken" and left frightened out of their wits, leaving all their equipment behind.

'In 1968 a Sussex Unidentified Flying Object research group held an all-night vigil at the ring. Sometime in the early hours of the morning one of the members walked around a clump of trees and became mysteriously paralyzed. Other members that rushed to their aid were also affected.

'Again in 1968 another UFO research group entered the ring and experienced a steep drop in temperature. Some of the members also experienced stomach cramps and difficulty breathing. They left the ring and their symptoms mysteriously disappeared.

'In 1972 a gentleman was walking over Chanctonbury with some friends. When they approached the ring they saw a flickering light inside and assumed someone had lit a fire. As they walked nearer, the light disappeared and the ring was deserted. From the centre of the ring they heard a loud swishing noise from above. They looked up and saw a large oblong-shaped object glowing red. Making no noise, the object moved away and shot up into the sky. An object of similar description was also witnessed in 1979.

'In 1974 a white, circular object was seen shooting up the west side of Chanctonbury Hill. It was reported to hover for just under a minute before changing to an oblong shape and disappearing to the north-west at great speed.

Again in 1974 some researchers were walking within the ring of trees when one of them was levitated about five feet off the floor by an unseen force for about sixty seconds.

'In 1975 a woman walking her dog at Chanctonbury saw a large, round, orange object land on Chanctonbury Hill. It stayed there for just under a minute before shooting up into the sky.

'In 1979 some researchers visited the ring. One of them found themselves knocked to the ground by an unseen force whilst another had their crucifix ripped from their neck and flung to the ground. When picked up they found it was twisted and hot to touch.'

It certainly seems that Chanctonbury Ring has much to offer not only the most avid of ghost hunters out there, but it also seems that watchers and researchers of Unidentified Flying Objects, UFOs, have a fair chance of witnessing something out of this world. What about the mysterious personal experiences that people report here. This is a phenomena that greatly interested me whilst researching this story and I have often wondered if there could be something natural, but perhaps not understood, that creates these unusual feelings and sensations of fear, panic and paralysis. But how on earth could you explain the phenomenon of levitation . . . and for such a prolonged time. Now that really does baffle me!

Not being able to offer any logical explanations for the events at Chanctonbury I turned once again to Stuart Logan for his closing thought on the ring, 'I have visited the ring on many occasions and at different times of the year; there is always a special feel to the place no matter when I visit, even on a warm summer day. Although I haven't got definite proof to put before people that the place has paranormal activity, I have no doubt in my mind that it has.'

CISSBURY RING, WORTHING, WEST SUSSEX

Cissbury Ring was allegedly created by mounds of earth that fell to the ground during the Devil's attempt to dig a large hole that would allow the sea to flood Sussex: obviously pure myth. What we do know is that humans have been using this area for thousands of years. The ring itself is an Iron Age hill fort dating back to around 250 BC and is the second largest hill fort in all of England; it spans some sixty acres. Underneath this hill fort lies even more history, for the remains of Stone Age flint mines, some extending to depths of forty feet, have also been discovered, along with human remains!

The main ghostly legend that hails from Cissbury Ring concerns a highwayman who was executed in the ring. As the highwayman was in his hour of death it is said that he uttered he would not rest following his execution. Perhaps he has lived up to his promise as some claim to have witnessed the spectral highwayman riding along on his steed.

CLAPHAM WOODS, CLAPHAM, WEST SUSSEX

The county of Sussex is deeply encased in many myths, legends and mysteries and none could be more enigmatic than the stories surrounding the haunting of Clapham Woods.

The wood is famed for its truly impressive beech tree, known as the 'Altar Tree', and also for many of the mysterious events that people allege have taken place here. There can be no doubt that something untoward has been going on in the woods in the past and a possible link to many of the phenomena experienced here could be attributed to an occult group known as the 'Friends of Hecate'.

Occult researcher Charles Walker has claimed he has encountered an individual of the Hecate clan who informed him that the woods were being used by the occult group and therefore issued a warning to him that his welfare would be at dire risk should his research and investigation into the occurrences at Clapham Woods continue. Mr Walker claims he has had numerous threats and has even had a gun pulled on him in order to warn him off his pursuit. Despite this, his research continues.

An occult pentagram found in Clapham woods by Stuart Logan. Even to this day these kinds of symbols appear frequently. Are they placed here by those practising witchcraft and dark arts or are they just a practical joke made in poor taste? © Stuart Logan

Unusual experiences at the woods were reported as early as the 1960s and many over the years claim to have witnessed Unidentified Flying Objects and mysterious spectral mists, and to have experienced sensations of unease, a feeling of being watched and sudden nausea. Dog walkers over the years claim their animals have exhibited sudden and irrational fear of certain areas of Clapham Woods and some even state their animals have disappeared into thin air: could these dogs have been taken by the Friends of Hecate? Hecate was an ancient goddess whose primary animal was the dog . . . might this be a connection?

Dogs disappearing, UFOs being seen and a plethora of other unusual occurrences are disturbing enough but none are more so than the four mysterious deaths that have occurred here. From 1972 through to 1981 there were a series of 'suspicious deaths' that happened in the area. The first came in 1972 when the remains of Police Constable Peter Goldsmith were discovered after he vanished whilst hiking; Leon Foster's body was discovered in 1975 after he had been missing for some weeks. The Reverend Harry Snelling, a former priest based at Clapham, vanished without trace in 1978; three years

The Sacred Beech Tree, also known as the Altar Tree, has been a focal point for many investigators looking into the mysterious events at Clapham Woods. © Stuart Logan

later his body was discovered. To date there has been no explanation or arrests concerning the deaths of these three individuals. The final collection of mortal remains was discovered in 1981. A woman who had been missing for six weeks, her name is commonly known but I feel it unethical to name her here, was found strangled after she had been subjected to sexual assault. Are all these deaths just a coincidence or have the stories of these persons' disappearances and subsequent suspicious deaths been embellished over the years to add to the enigma of Clapham Woods?

In 2004 I was treated to a short expedition to the woods with Paranormal and Occult researcher Stuart Logan. Stuart has spent countless hours researching and investigating the woods and has had some strange experiences here which he is happy to relate once more to the readers of *Paranormal Sussex*. He recollects, 'One sensitive who was with us when entering the area got a smack in the face and another sensitive was so affected by what was there that when they went back to their car they thought the steering wheel had been taken from their car. They were disorientated and did not register which side of the road they should be driving on . . . however, this effect disappeared once we were about a mile from the location.

'We have encountered a strange force near the tree. Three of my friends (all sensitives) were sitting on the log near the tree when, as a whole, all three suddenly shot up and moved quickly away from the log. When questioned about what had made them move they had all felt like there was a force coming up behind them and they all reacted to it at exactly the same time.

'Another time up at the tree I was sitting down the path towards the field and the rest of the group were at the tree. We all then heard what sounded like a woman screaming, but unfortunately there is no 100 per cent way of proving it was not another person in the wood but it certainly did not sound very natural, almost like a last scream you do before being killed.'

Many intrepid investigators still make their way to Clapham Woods to this day, some even camping out for a number of days and nights, in the hope of drawing some conclusions to the mysteries of the woods and discovering what really is going on here. If you go down to these woods today . . . you could be in for a very supernatural surprise!

COACH AND HORSES, ST PANCRAS, CHICHESTER, WEST SUSSEX

Being a ghost hunter, paranormal researcher and all-round supernatural obsessive for some twenty-odd years has meant that I have inevitably built up quite a collection of ghost-related literature and other sources of media. One of my particular favorites for sourcing stories of lesser known origins is my collection of press clippings from various areas around the UK.

Back in December 2003 there was a rather interesting article that appeared in the *Chichester Observer* concerning one of the city's ghosts. The haunting takes place in the Coach and Horses Public House in St Pancras. One of the most recent eyewitness accounts of this ghost was made by teacher Richard Marsden who was drinking and talking to the landlord when he noticed a sudden rush of cold air, a phenomenon that was experienced by at least two other people at the same time. Looking up Mr Marsden was somewhat shocked to see the ghost of a woman who was moving, at a rapid speed, through the pub and appeared to be clutching a bundle in her arms, some have speculated this mysterious bundle is in fact the lady's baby.

Descriptions of the phantom woman are that she has a long grey dress which appears to be of hessian-cloth, that is tied at the waist, long dark hair and what appears to be some kind of jewelry around her neck which has been likened to a choker.

COMET STORE, WORTHING, WEST SUSSEX

A modern-day shopping store retailing the latest in electronic gadgetry and wizardry is not the usual run-of-the-mill place in which one would expect to discover a haunting. Come to the Comet store in Worthing and you may see a little more than your next television set!

Worthing has a long history and there is archaeological evidence which suggests that mankind has lived in this region since prehistoric times, although the site which the Comet Store now occupies appears not to have any major, strong links to the past. Many people think that in order to have a haunting and a ghost you need an old, rambling mansion, preferable where some horrific deeds have been committed, but this is not the case in all instances and in many circumstances the history of the land in which the place is sited can be more relevant to a haunting than the buildings themselves.

The Comet store has no past history, apart from being a shop belonging to a major high street supermarket chain, but there is a tragic history connected with this relatively young building. It's a hot spot for suicides with at least three deaths occurring here in recent years. Staff working at the store have reported a series of unexplained events including footsteps, boxes being moved on their own, sensations of apprehension and fear and even feeling as if you have been brushed past. It's all these unexplainable events that eventually led to the Paranormal Investigation Group Sussex, www.the-pigs.co.uk, being called in to investigate the reported phenomenon. Investigation Coordinator Tim Brown told me about his investigation at the store: 'Our investigation took place in early October 2008; the original idea was to raise money for the Make a Wish charity by letting the staff take part for a donation to the charity. We thought that we would collect no evidence to back up any of the claims, however, it has to be said that we did collect some strange things on the night. We filmed a black shadow walking across the warehouse, the reason we will not present this as evidence is because we can't be sure where all of the people were in the building at the time and it's possible that somebody may have walked in front of the infrared flood lighting we used on the night, casting an infrared shadow. We also have video footage from one of the teams where a strange, long, almost floating light, could be seen in the upper warehouse but again we can't be sure if this is a reflection from something else and thus we have not put it forward as evidence. There was a strange EMF fluctuation on the shop floor which appeared to change on command; however, as you can imagine, the building is full of electromagnetic fields.'

If the team from Paranormal Investigation Group Sussex are prepared to look at this haunting in a rational and logical fashion, as they have done, and dismiss their evidence as they cannot be 100 per cent certain it's paranormal in origin, then is there anything else that could warrant further investigation? . . . apparently so!

Since the Paranormal Investigation Group Sussex conducted their investigation in 2008, the manager of the store, Mike Burrows, contacted them reporting yet more weird and wonderful occurrences. 'During the following month after our visit the store manager was called by the alarm company to alert him that the inside movement sensors had detected movement in the upper warehouse area. The store manager arrived at the store at about 12.30 a.m. accompanied by two police officers. They entered the store and made their way to the upper warehouse where they found an inner door was wide open. This door has to be shut and bolted before the alarm can be set in the evening. The police officers searched the store for intruders but since there were no signs of any forced entry to the store and nobody could be found inside the building they locked up the store again. The store manager then found that he couldn't reset the alarm so he called the alarm company who told him that the movement sensors were picking up somebody walking about in the upper warehouse area. Once again the police officers and the store manager made their way back to the upper warehouse to find that once again the inner door had been opened and the skin of the door had come away from the main part of the door. Again the area was searched and nobody could be found and no signs of forced entry or exit were detected. They all decided to leave and secure the building. The store manager, who is sceptical about the existence of the paranormal, mentioned to the police officers about the possibility of a haunting which they found greatly amusing. Since that incident the reports of movement and footsteps have continued.'

CONNAUGHT THEATRE, WORTHING, WEST SUSSEX

The Connaught theatre was built in 1914 and was originally known as the picturedrome. The Connaught became a fully fledged theatre when members of the Worthing Repertory Company acquired the building back in 1935. Since that time the venue has become a favourite theatre amongst many of the locals and also a two-screen cinema showing some of the latest block-buster movie releases.

In the excellent 1988 book *Theatre Ghosts* by Roy Harley Lewis, there is a story concerning the ghost of a woman, whom some say is dressed in Elizabethan clothing whereas others claim it to be Victorian, who has been seen wandering the confines of the theatre. The book details the last of these sightings to be in August 1987 when fifteen-year-old Joseph Hall walked straight into the path of the ghost on the theatre's spiral staircase whilst retrieving something from underneath the stage. Was this ghost still treading the boards at this theatre, I thought? . . . only one way to find out!

I spoke to Rosie Gray, a theatre employee, who told me 'I have heard of sightings here in the past and it really interests me but unfortunately I have never seen anything myself. One of the staff members did claim to see "something" move towards the rear of the theatre and then see the curtains move on their own but we don't know what that could have been.' So the ghost is long gone then?

'Back in 2007 we had two carpet layers in the theatre and one of the gentleman came up to theatre manager saying that he had just seen the ghost of a woman sporting a 1930s hairstyle and he wanted to know if the theatre was haunted. His friend also claims to have seen the same ghost.' This is starting to get interesting. Does the ghost at the Connaught change with the times, what with being mentioned as Elizabethan, Victorian and now 1930s, or could there actually be more ghosts at this place than initially suspected? Hopefully future investigations will reveal many more supernatural goings-on at the theatre.

COWDRAY HOUSE, MIDHURST, WEST SUSSEX

Cowdray House is now nothing more than ruins but it stands as a testament to what greatness this house once boasted. The house was constructed around the sixteenth century and its history is a veritable who's who of visitors both famous and infamous, Henry VIII being one visitor in particular who visited the castle on a number of occasions.

Despite the house's, and indeed the family's, high status, it could not assure them of an easy life and in 1538 a dispossessed monk from Battle Abbey cursed the family 'by fire and by water' after Anthony Browne, a member of the Fitzwilliam family who owned Cowdray, was given Battle Abbey. Curses are an integral part of British folklore and history and to come across one that appears to be true (well, maybe) is an interesting turn of events.

I spoke to Heather Ongley, who is the operations manager of the Cowdray Heritage Trust, who was able to tell me some more about the curse that befell the Fitzwilliam Family. 'The events of 1793 were said to have fulfilled a dreadful curse uttered 250 years earlier when Henry VIII gave Battle Abbey in East Sussex to Sir Anthony Browne after the dissolution. The King kept the plate and jewels for himself but the furnishings were sold and the abbot and the brethren were dismissed on pensions. Sir Anthony demolished the abbey church and the monks' accommodation, keeping the abbot's sumptuous lodgings for himself and building a great wing intended, but never used, to house the young Princess Elizabeth, whose guardian he was.

'The monks regarded the abbey's destruction and their expulsion as acts of sacrilege. One day, when Sir Anthony and Lady Browne were feasting, one of the monks strode into the hall and approached to curse the interlopers at length. He foretold the doom that would fall upon their descendants and prophesied that a curse would cling to the family until it ceased to exist. He

Cowdray House, near Midhurst, is a place touched by tragedy and a curse that brought down an entire family line . . . a perfect place to search for ghosts! Photo © Cowdray Heritage Trust

shouted, 'By fire and by water thy line shall come to an end and it shall perish out of the land.'

It took two and a half centuries before the curse took effect but, perhaps or perhaps not coincidentally, it was fire and the waters of the Rhine that brought about the downfall of the family. On 24 September 1793 the house burnt down in a huge fire sparked by a workman's brazier left overnight. Workmen were redecorating the house in readiness for the Viscount's wedding. Meanwhile, the twenty-four-year-old Viscount was on holiday in Germany with his friend, and they decided to run the rapids at Laufenburg. Despite locals' warnings of danger, they set off and the boat overturned in the rapids and they both drowned. So the house was burned down and the childless Viscount was drowned within two weeks of each other. It is rumoured that a

The ruins of Cowdray House where the ghost of one of its former owners, the 5th Viscount Montague, and his wife still haunt to this very day. Mysterious wet footsteps on the tower staircase and a child's disembodied voice have also been experienced here. Photo © Cowdray Heritage Trust

servant from Cowdray, on his way to tell the Viscount of the house's burning, spotted another Cowdray servant at Calais, on his way back to Sussex to tell the household of the Viscount's demise.

It did not end in 1793. The young Viscount's sister inherited the Cowdray estates, married and had two young sons. In the summer of 1815 the family were on holiday at Bognor and, one afternoon, her husband took the boys on a boating trip. A sudden squall blew up, the little vessel overturned and both boys were drowned, not far from the shore and in front of their watching mother. Cowdray had been devastated, the young Viscount drowned without heirs and his sister's boys also drowned.'

Was a curse at work on the family, was it just coincidence or could it have been just rotten, bad luck that reared its ugly head on the Fitzwilliams? So what is it that haunts here? Despite working at Cowdray for some time now, Heather openly admits that she has 'never seen or heard anything myself' but knows of others who have, including one group of people who were recently investigating the ghosts of Cowdray and allegedly became aware of the presence of Anne Boleyn. Unfortunately there are no records of Anne Boleyn ever visiting Cowdray Castle, but does this mean the intrepid ghost hunters are wrong?

Heather told me more of the houses hauntings. 'The most common one is a grey or white lady walking from Midhurst town towards Cowdray House. This is purported to be the wife of the 5th Viscount Montague. He apparently shot a priest dead in the chapel here at Cowdray for starting the Mass without him in 1702. The Viscount fled to the keeper's lodge and hid in a six-foot-square priest hole until he died in 1717. He would only come out for an hour at midnight when his wife would bring him food and other comforts. If this story is true, it is likely that locals saw a lady walking to the keeper's lodge in a grey cape. It may be that they thought she was a ghost. It is said she wore a long white dress so that people would think she was a ghost and this would deter onlookers – obviously they did not want him to be found while he was in hiding. After their deaths, there was talk of two ghosts, one of the Viscount himself whose troubled spirit was said to haunt the room until the house burnt down in 1793, and then his wife is said to float down 'lady's walk' on summer evenings, which is a walkway further up the hill towards the new Cowdray House where Lord and Lady Cowdray live. The white or grey lady has been the one most commonly seen in the twentieth and twenty-first centuries.

'As for other experiences, on a recent ghost hunt by a private company, one lady felt a malevolent presence of a man in our wine cellar. One of our volunteers hears a child say "hello" very boldly in our gatehouse when no one else is around. Another one states there are presences in the pantry, and yet another one has seen wet footprints on the steps to the tower, when no one had been in the tower, let alone with wet feet.'

Within the confines of Cowdray House we have a classic ghost story, tales of tragedy and, of course, not forgetting a legendary curse. This place is a real gem of a find in terms of a location to investigate and mysteries to unravel.

If you would like to visit Cowdray House for yourself then please do contact the trust at the details below:

Cowdray Heritage Trust Visitor Centre:
River Ground Stables
Cowdray Park
Midhurst
West Sussex
GU29 9AL
Tel: 01730 810781 or email: info@cowdray.org.uk

The beautiful house that is Cuckfield Park. Photo © Peregrine Bryant

CUCKFIELD PARK, CUCKFIELD, WEST SUSSEX

Cuckfield village has been known to me for some twenty-odd years now because of two stories that interested me a great deal in my early years. The first one is the story of Geranium Jane, a fantastic ghost story where a poor lady was murdered by having her head caved in with a large pot of geraniums (see the story about the Kings Head Public House in Cuckfield for more information on this), and the second story, not paranormal I hasten to add, concerns a gentleman by the name of Gideon Mantell (1790-1852) who discovered the first fossilised remains of a dinosaur, that we now know as iguanodon, in the village.

During the sixteenth century Henry and Elizabeth Bowyer decided to build a new home for themselves on the site of an old medieval hall. After the demolition of the old hall was completed, the construction of a new house, known at the time

43

The gateway to
Cuckfield Park. Photo
© Peregrine Bryant

as Cuckfield Place but now called Cuckfield Park, was commenced and completed
around 1574. Cuckfield Park remained in the ownership of the Bowyer family for
over 115 years until the house was sold to a Mr Charles Sergison in 1691. It is from
the Sergison family that the haunting of Cuckfield Park stems.

In 1848 the lady of the house, Mrs Ann Sergison, passed away at the age
of eighty-five years old. By all accounts Mrs Sergison had quite a bad temper
and soon after her death there were reports of her ghost being seen both
inside Cuckfield Park and also in the grounds. One story states she was even
witnessed swinging on the gates of Cuckfield Park; this obviously caused
some concern and three church goers decided to perform an exorcism of Mrs
Sergison's ghost and apparently drowned the restless wraith in the font. How
one could achieve this task is beyond me! Personally, if she was seen haunting
the house and park soon after her death with witnesses often thinking the

ghost was actually a real person as she was so lifelike, then I think she is still around. Perhaps lying low so nobody else tries to drown her.

The park is also home to a bizarre phenomenon, if it can be proven to be a phenomenon at all that is, for it is said that when a member of the family that owns Cuckfield Park dies there is a self-amputating tree that will drop one of its branches . . . question is, how do you know which tree to look at when one of the family is about to die?

DEANS PLACE HOTEL, ALFRISTON, EAST SUSSEX

If you happen to be staying at the Deans Place Hotel and fancy an evening walk around the lanes that surround the hotel then be sure to keep an eye out for the phantom dog that has been reported wandering the lanes and roads in the area. Some witnesses claim the spectral hound is white whilst others state it is black; considering the vast difference in the reported colour of the dog, could there actually be two separate ghostly dogs? Have people misinterpreted what they have seen or is this simply an urban legend? One thing is for sure with this ghost though, it hasn't been reported for some time now.

The hotel also has a ghost that has not been seen for some time. From the eighteenth to the nineteenth century there were sporadic reports of a mysterious spectral blue lady who had been encountered at the hotel, once even pushing past a guest who was staying at the hotel. Local legend, and probably just a myth, tells us that many years ago a woman was murdered and her body was hidden in a settle on the landing. Unfortunately this story has never been confirmed using historical record so it is impossible to state for sure whether this is a true story or not. The Blue Lady has not been seen at Deans Place Hotel since the 1970s, and what with the recent modernisation of the hotel, perhaps this ghost has finally been laid to rest, but I guess only time will reveal this for sure!

DEVONSHIRE PARK THEATRE, EASTBOURNE, EAST SUSSEX

The ghost of a phantom violin player has been reported at this nineteenth-century theatre. Unlike many stories where witnesses of ghostly encounters report misty and transparent apparitions, the people who have reported seeing the spectral musician, dressed in black tails, bow tie, white shirt and carrying his violin and bow, state that he is very lifelike and very solid. In fact, the very real, lifelike appearance of the ghost has led many people to believe he is in fact a member of the land of the living and it is only when he vanishes in front of the very eyes of the

The photo is taken by Helen Benzie at the Devonshire Park Theatre, Eastbourne. Many people claim to be able to see the spectre of a female dressed in Victorian clothing. Is it a ghost, wishful thinking or an optical illusion? Photo © Helen Benzie of the Sussex Paranormal Research Group.

witnesses concerned, or no trace can be found of a person, that people realise that they have witnessed something altogether a little more unworldly.

Paranormal Investigator Helen Benzie was part of an investigation that took place at the Devonshire Park Theatre, an investigation in which the participants were hoping to discover more about the ghostly violinist. The investigation, however, did not reveal anything about the known ghost but a photo taken by Helen appears to show what many believe to be a woman in Victorian clothing.

FISHERMAN'S JOY, EAST STREET, SELSEY, WEST SUSSEX

The sleepy little Sussex village of Selsey is today renowned as the residence of the world-famous amateur astronomer, and all-round British living legend, Sir Patrick Moore. Sir Patrick is known for his world-record-breaking TV show *The*

The Fisherman's Joy Public House in East Street, Selsey. Did a fire here in days gone by claim the lives of a family who may still haunt their former residence?

Sky at Night, authoring over 100 books and being the greatest spokesperson for astronomy that has probably ever lived. The town is also home to a haunted pub, the Fisherman's Joy, in East Street.

Sitting at a junction, nestled between housing, lies the public house that used to be a main stopping off point for holidaymakers *en route* to the old Pontins holiday camp, a holiday camp that is now long gone. The pub is home to at least two ghosts that have been seen by mere normal, everyday folk; there does, however, appear to be more here to witness should you be of a psychic inclination.

I spoke to Kerry Chadwick, the current owner's daughter and a barmaid at the pub, who said, 'We have before, in the past, heard the sounds of the bar stools scraping across the wooden floor and the sounds of glasses clinking. There isn't anyone down here as the pub is usually closed when this happens. People have reported seeing the ghost of a little girl and also a black shadow that moves across, from the left to right when viewed from the bar, in front of the main entrance and then vanishes through the window where the original doorway once was.'

The main corridor leading to the restaurant and toilet area of the Fisherman's Joy Public House. It has been in this corridor that the ghostly girl has been witnessed most frequently.

So who is this little girl, I thought? Could Kerry give me an answer as to the child's identity and perhaps even an explanation for why the girl remains here? 'Some time ago we had a psychic investigator pay a visit to the pub and they claimed to be able to see the ghost of a man, a young boy, a woman and the little girl. They said that the woman was warning them of a fire at the pub in which the lives of her family were taken. The little girl that has been seen here was the daughter of the woman and she perished here. In fact, out of the family of four, only the woman survived the blaze. Unfortunately we have not been able to confirm a fire in the historical record of the pub,' said Kerry.

FORD AIRFIELD, FORD, WEST SUSSEX

This former airfield, an RAF station used in the Battle of Britain during the Second World War, is now more associated with the thriving market and car-boot sales that are held here than its historical past. Indeed the market and car-boot sales are so popular the Ford Airfield Market website states quite proudly that it is 'open 52 weeks of the year "rain or shine"'. Being associated with the military it is no surprise to discover that some people, walking on the field, have reported encountering past members of the armed forces. The ghost of an old-style airman carrying his parachute has been reported here.

FOREDOWN TOWER, PORTSLADE, EAST SUSSEX

In the 1997 book *Haunted Sussex Today*, which was written by acclaimed ghost hunter and paranormal author and researcher Andrew Green, there is a story concerning a ghost that allegedly haunts the Foredown Tower in Portslade. Mr Green's article relates to the reader, 'Early in 1992 one or two members of the staff reported that they felt that they were being watched by someone or something unseen, and inexplicable sounds would be heard. The security alarm would go off for no reason and for which no explanation could be found. In April of that year footsteps were heard walking up and down an area of the first floor.'

During the course of researching *Paranormal Sussex* I was lucky enough to find the person who claims to have heard the footsteps, a first-hand eyewitness to the phenomenon. Great, I thought, or until we discussed the matter further and was told by the person, who wished to remain anonymous, 'the comments were very much "off the cuff" and said in a youthful spirit of misadventure which I now regret – and were "worked up into a plausible story" by Andrew Green. Quite simply, they are not true. As also reported in the book, the fire alarms did go off regularly but the system always suffered faults, most likely from the building being damp or other environmental reasons. The "footsteps heard walking up and down" were also reported by me and I did indeed "hear" such through the video link with the upper floors but I am 100 per cent convinced this was via a "trick of the ear" or had environmental causes. Again, this story was taken as fact and possibly elaborated on by the author and should not be taken as evidence of the paranormal – that would be foolish in my opinion.'

Paula Wrightson, an employee of the tower who has worked here for many years commented that 'reports of Foredown Tower being haunted are simply untrue. I worked at Foredown full-time from 1991 to 2004 (and have been closely involved since then) and not once did I have a spooky experience. I also know of no other people who have had such experiences there. In fact Foredown Tower has a pleasant atmosphere and is a lovely building in which to spend time. I would certainly not say it is haunted in any shape or form.

Foredown Tower in Portslade. The site of a haunting which can now be laid to rest following the publication of this book. Photo © Paula Wrightson.

It may seem unusual to carry a story in a book about ghosts about a place that is not really haunted but in my other works, *Paranormal Hampshire* and *Paranormal Wiltshire*, it has started to become quite a common feature of mine to expose untruths and misconceived information about certain hauntings. Why is this you may ask? Simple. Would you want to go ghost hunting in a place where there is actually no ghost present? Neither would I and that's the reason why this story is recorded here in *Paranormal Sussex*. It's time to put this story to bed and move onto researching real, or at least allegedly real, haunted places.

GLYDWISH WOODS, NR BURWASH, EAST SUSSEX

Glydwish Woods is a well known spot to both locals of the area and also to paranormal enthusiasts, for the woods are allegedly haunted.

In the nineteenth century a gentleman by the name of David Leaney took lodgings with one Benjamin Russell and his wife. One night Russell suggested an illicit hunting trip in Glydwish woods. Separating for a short while whilst engaging in a little spot of poaching, it is claimed that Leaney heard a crash in the woods and he went to see what had happened. Leaney found his friend and landlord, Benjamin, lying on the ground . . . dead!

A doctor was summoned, and as suggested by some, not a very competent one. He gave the cause of death as arsenic poisoning, which was probably influenced by local gossip that had spread throughout the area that Leaney was romantically involved with Russell's wife.

Leaney was found guilty of murder at his trial and the death penalty was duly handed out. Leaney always protested his innocence and said, before the hangman did his job, that he would return to haunt all those that had placed him in the position of now losing his own life. Further examination of Benjamin Russell's body revealed he had actually died from a heart attack. Mrs Russell was released from her incarceration but by the time the true cause of death was established, it was already too late for poor old David Leaney.

People over the years claim to have seen the spectre, often thought to be that of Leaney, wandering through the woods wearing ragged clothes and clutching at his throat.

GOODWOOD HOUSE, CHICHESTER, WEST SUSSEX

Goodwood House is today famed for its horse racing and its annual motor racing event, The Festival of Speed. The house has been the seat of the Dukes of Richmond since 1697 and is still stated to be very much a family home.

The ghost or ghosts that may, or may not, haunt here cause much confusion. There is only one vague reference to the Duchess of Richmond making a comment that a guest should be accommodated in the haunted room. However, we do not know where this room was or even what allegedly haunts it. It appears the whole basis of the story saying that Goodwood is haunted in the first place could come from a very famous paranormal writer and enthusiast, Charles Dickens. Mr Dickens apparently wrote *The Goodwood Ghost Story*, which is entirely fictional, but many think it's a true story telling of a possible ghost at Goodwood House. I now reproduce the story that is attributed to Charles Dickens so the reader can fully understand the haunting at Goodwood House:

My wife's sister, Mrs M—, was left a widow at the age of thirty-five, with two children, girls, of whom she was passionately fond. She carried on the draper's business at Bognor, established by her husband. Being still a very handsome woman, there were several suitors for her hand. The only favoured one amongst them was a Mr Barton. My wife never liked this Mr Barton, and made no secret of her feelings to her sister, whom she frequently told that Mr Barton only wanted to be master of the little haberdashery shop in Bognor. He was a man in poor circumstances, and had no other motive in his proposal of marriage, so my wife thought, than to better himself.

On the 23rd of August 1831 Mrs M— arranged to go with Barton to a picnic party at Goodwood Park, the seat of the Duke of Richmond, who had kindly thrown open his grounds to the public for the day. My wife, a little annoyed at her going out with this man, told her she had much better remain at home to look after her children and attend to the business. Mrs M—, however, bent on going, made arrangements about leaving the shop, and got my wife to promise to see to her little girls while she was away.

The party set out in a four-wheeled phaeton, with a pair of ponies driven by Mrs M—, and a gig for which I lent the horse.

Now we did not expect them to come back till nine or ten o'clock, at any rate. I mention this particularly to show that there could be no expectation of their earlier return in the mind of my wife, to account for what follows.

At six o'clock that bright summer's evening my wife went out into the garden to call the children. Not finding them, she went all round the place in her search till she came to the empty stable; thinking they might have run in there to play, she pushed open the door; there, standing in the darkest corner, she saw Mrs M—. My wife was surprised to see her, certainly; for she did not expect her return so soon; but, oddly enough, it did not strike her as being singular to see her there. Vexed as she had felt with her all day for going, and rather glad, in her woman's way, to have something entirely different from the genuine *casus belli* to hang a retort upon, my wife said: 'Well, Harriet, I should have thought another dress would have done quite as well for your picnic as that best black silk you have on.' My wife was the elder of the twain, and had always assumed a little of the air of counsellor to her sister. Black silks were thought a great deal more of at that time than they are just now, and silk of any kind was held particularly inconsistent wear for Wesleyan Methodists, to which denomination we belonged.

Receiving no answer, my wife said: 'Oh, well, Harriet, if you can't take a word of reproof without being sulky, I'll leave you to yourself'; and then she came into the house to tell me the party had returned and that she had seen her sister in the stable, not in the best of tempers. At the moment it did not seem extraordinary to me that my wife should have met her sister in the stable.

I waited indoors some time, expecting them to return my horse. Mrs M— was my neighbour, and, being always on most friendly terms, I wondered that none of the party had come in to tell us about the day's pleasure. I thought I would just run in and see how they had got on. To my great surprise the servant told me they had not returned. I began, then, to feel anxiety about the result. My wife, however, having seen Harriet in the stable, refused to believe the servant's assertion; and said there was no doubt of their return, but that they had probably left word to say they were not come back, in order to offer a plausible excuse for taking a further drive, and detaining my horse for another hour or so.

At eleven o'clock Mr Pinnock, my brother-in-law, who had been one of the party, came in, apparently much agitated. As soon as she saw him, and before he had time to speak, my wife seemed to know what he had to say.

'What is the matter?' she said; 'something has happened to Harriet, I know!'

'Yes' replied Mr Pinnock; 'if you wish to see her alive, you must come with me directly to Goodwood.'

From what he said it appeared that one of the ponies had never been properly broken in; that the man from whom the turn-out was hired for the day had cautioned Mrs M— respecting it before they started; and that he had lent it reluctantly, being the only pony to match in the stable at the time, and would not have lent it at all had he not known Mrs M— to be a remarkably good whip.

On reaching Goodwood, it seems, the gentlemen of the party had got out, leaving the ladies to take a drive round the park in the phaeton. One or both of the ponies must then have taken fright at something in the road, for Mrs M— had scarcely taken the reins when the ponies shied. Had there been plenty of room she would readily have mastered the difficulty; but it was in a narrow road, where a gate obstructed the way. Some men rushed to open the gate – too late. The three other ladies jumped out at the beginning of the accident; but Mrs M— still held on to the reins, seeking to control her ponies, until, finding it was impossible for the men to get the gate open in time, she too sprang forward; and at the same instant the ponies came smash on to the gate. She had made her spring too late, and fell heavily to the ground on her head. The heavy, old-fashioned comb of the period, with which her hair was looped up, was driven into her skull by the force of the fall. The Duke of Richmond, a witness to the accident, ran to her assistance, lifted her up, and rested her head upon his knees. The only words Mrs M— had spoken were uttered at the time: 'Good God, my children!' By direction of the Duke she was immediately conveyed to a neighbouring inn, where every assistance, medical and otherwise, that forethought or kindness could suggest was afforded her.

At six o'clock in the evening, the time at which my wife had gone into the stable and seen what we now knew had been her spirit, Mrs M—, in her sole interval of returning consciousness, had made a violent but unsuccessful attempt to speak. From her glance having wandered round the room, in solemn awful wistfulness, it had been conjectured she wished to see some relative or friend not then present. I went to Goodwood in the gig with Mr Pinnock, and arrived in time to see my sister-in-law die at two o'clock in the morning. Her only conscious moments had been those in which she laboured unsuccessfully to speak, which had occurred at six o'clock. She wore a black silk dress.

When we came to dispose of her business, and to wind up her affairs, there was scarcely anything left for the two orphan girls. Mrs M—'s father, however, being well-to-do, took them to bring up. At his death, which happened soon afterwards, his property went to his eldest son, who speedily dissipated the inheritance. During a space of two years the children were taken as visitors by various relations in turn, and lived an unhappy life with no settled home.

For some time I had been debating with myself how to help these children, having many boys and girls of my own to provide for. I had almost settled to take them myself, bad as trade was with me, at the time, and bring them up with my own family, when one day business called me to Brighton. The business was so urgent that it necessitated my travelling at night.

I set out from Bognor in a close-headed gig on a beautiful moonlight winter's night, when the crisp frozen snow lay deep over the earth, and its fine glistening dust was whirled about in little eddies on the bleak night-wind – driven now and then in stinging powder against my tingling cheek, warm and glowing in the sharp air. I had taken my great 'Bose' (short for 'Boatswain') for company. He lay, blinking wakefully, sprawled out on the spare seat of the gig beneath a mass of warm rugs.

Between Littlehampton and Worthing is a lonely piece of road, long and dreary, through bleak and bare open country, where the snow lay knee-deep, sparkling in the moonlight. It was so cheerless that I turned round to speak to my dog, more for the sake of hearing the sound of a voice than anything else. 'Good Bose,' I said, patting him, 'there's a good dog!' Then suddenly I noticed he shivered, and shrank underneath the wraps. Then the horse required my attention, for he gave a start, and was going wrong, and had nearly taken me into the ditch.

Then I looked up. Walking at my horse's head, dressed in a sweeping robe, so white that it shone dazzling against the white snow, I saw a lady, her back turned to me, her head bare; her hair dishevelled and strayed, showing sharp and black against her white dress.

I was at first so much surprised at seeing a lady, so dressed, exposed to the open night, and such a night as this, that I scarcely knew what to do. Recovering myself, I called out to know if I could render assistance – if she wished to ride? No answer. I drove faster, the horse blinking, and shying, and trembling the while, his ears laid back in abject terror. Still the figure maintained its position close to my horse's head. Then I thought that what I saw was no woman, but perchance a man disguised for the purpose of robbing me, seeking an opportunity to seize the bridle and stop the horse. Filled with this idea, I said, 'Good Bose! hi! look at it, boy!' but the dog only shivered as if in fright. Then we came to a place where four cross-roads meet.

Determined to know the worst, I pulled up the horse. I fetched Bose, unwilling, out by the ears. He was a good dog at anything from a rat to a man, but he slunk away that night into the hedge, and lay there, his head between his paws, whining and howling. I walked straight up to the figure, still standing by the horse's head. As I walked, the figure turned, and I saw Harriet's face as plainly as I see you now – white and calm – placid, as idealised and beautified by death. I must own that, though not a nervous man, in that instant I felt sick and faint. Harriet looked me full in the face with a long, eager, silent look. I knew then it was her spirit, and felt a strange calm come over me, for I knew it was nothing to harm me. When I could speak, I asked what troubled her. She looked at me still, never changing that cold fixed stare. Then I felt in my mind it was her children, and I said:

'Harriet! is it for your children you are troubled?'

No answer.

'Harriet,' I continued, 'if for these you are troubled, be assured they shall never want while I have power to help them. Rest in peace!'

Still no answer.

I put up my hand to wipe from my forehead the cold perspiration which had gathered there. When I took my hand away from shading my eyes, the figure was gone. I was alone on the bleak snow-covered ground. The breeze, that had been hushed before, breathed coolly and gratefully on my face, and the cold stars glimmered and sparkled sharply in the far blue heavens. My dog crept up to me and furtively licked my hand, as who would say, 'Good master, don't be angry. I have served you in all but this.'

I took the children and brought them up till they could help themselves.

So could the ghost that haunts Goodwood House be the legendary Charles Dickens's sister-in-law, who was taken so tragically in an awful accident? I made my own enquiries at Goodwood House about their ghost and was told by the curator of the Goodwood Collection, Rosemary Baird, 'We do not have any records of hauntings here at Goodwood.' The question of what haunted room the Duchess of Richmond once remarked on remains a mystery!

HAYES HOTEL, NORTHIAM, EAST SUSSEX

This fifteenth-century building, which is a charming hotel, is the home to the ghost of an old lady who has been seen sitting at a spinning wheel in the hotel. There is also a story connected to a former owner of the house, Molly Beale. Molly was being forced to leave her husband by the gentleman with whom she was having an affair. When the man's desires were not fulfilled, he killed Molly. There have been reports of people witnessing the apparition of a lady from a short distance and a former landlady had a near face to face encounter with the ghost of a 'young lady aged about thirty, wearing a white hat and a grey dress'. There is also a legend about the murder of a baker's daughter at the hotel that is alleged to have occurred here in the 1970s. I can announce with pleasure, though, that this legend is just a myth. I spoke to an employee at the hotel, who wished to remain anonymous, and he said, 'The murder of the baker's daughter is complete rubbish. We have had people say they have seen a ghost here but I have slept numerous times in the room myself where Molly was murdered and have never had an experience.' If you would like to try your hand at bearing witness to the ghost of the phantom lady sitting at the spinning wheel or perhaps even Molly herself then why not book yourself in for a spooky sleepover. Remember to ask for the room in which Molly was murdered; it's called the Molly Beale Room!

HERSTMONCEUX CASTLE, HAILSHAM, EAST SUSSEX

Herstmonceux Castle is one of the county's stately gems that most people look at *en route* to an alternative event or destination, mainly one of the many events that celebrate one of the world's oldest sciences, astronomy, for Herstmonceux is also home to the Royal Greenwich Observatory.

The building was constructed in 1441 for Roger Fiennes, who was at the time Treasurer of the Household for King Henry VI, and was designed to be a place that instantly conveyed a 'wow' factor. The castle was never meant to serve as a defensive structure and was purely a status symbol. Herstmonceux castle has had many owners over the years but in 1946 it was sold to the Admiralty so that the castle's grounds could be put to work for the use of the Royal Greenwich Observatory. The observatory remained at Herstmonceux until it was eventually moved to Cambridge in 1988. Despite this the observatory is a popular science centre and many events, fairs, lectures and exhibitions popularising astronomy continue to this day.

The castle is home to a fair few spectres. There is the ghost of a grey lady who is said to have been starved to death and now haunts the corridors of the castle; people claim to have not only witnessed the ghost but to also have heard her painful sobbing. A ghost of a lady, known as the white lady, has been seen around the outside of the castle. It is claimed that Roger Fiennes abused and subsequently murdered the girl but another story relates the tale that the young lady actually drowned herself in the moat so as to avoid the amorous advances of the lustful Fiennes. If you should happen to see a woman riding a white donkey, then by all means take the time to take a second glance as the woman might not be from the land of the living, for a ghost answering this description has also been reported.

Next we come to the most famous ghost that haunts Herstmonceux Castle. Lord Dacre was said to have loudly beaten on his drum in order to ward off potential love rivals that were showing an interest in his considerably younger wife. Eventually, Dacre's wife became so annoyed at this that she locked Lord Dacre into a room and starved him to death. Could it be the ghost of Lord Dacre who has been seen walking the battlements, standing at nine foot tall, beating a drum and producing a shower of sparks?

Herstmonceux Castle has the ghost of a nine-foot-tall drummer, spectral women, an animal and even a sleep-walking man amongst its repertoire of supernatural inhabitants.

The last ghost that has been witnessed here is the wraith of a sleepwalking man! I have often pondered the theory that this ghost was a man who passed from this mortal realm in his sleep and now haunts the castle, blissfully unaware of what transpired during his slumber.

HM PRISON LEWES, LEWES, EAST SUSSEX

This Victorian prison was constructed in 1853 and has a capacity to hold over 700 inmates. Originally its cells were used to house prisoners of the Crimean War but many have since passed through its gates including notable figures such as Eamon de Valera (1882-1975), a former president of Ireland, and George Ramsdale Witton (1874-1942), a lieutenant in the Bushveldt Carbineers during the Boer War in South Africa who was convicted for the murder of prisoners of war. Unfortunately the ghost haunting this prison is no one famous enough to be easily identified. The phantom of a Victorian woman has been seen but no one knows who she is or why she haunts such a place . . . I could think of much better places to spend an eternity but whatever it is that binds her here remains a complete mystery.

HOLY TRINITY CHURCH, BOSHAM, WEST SUSSEX

This quaint little church in the parish of Bosham is easily missed but do pop in and have a look around if you are able to, for this place of worship has a very interesting tale to tell. For many years now there has been some speculation that the unidentified human remains found under the chancel arch in the 1950s belong to none other than Harold Godwinson, the King of England who was defeated and killed at the Battle of Hastings in 1066.

It's claimed that Harold's men whisked his body away from the battlefield in order to carry out a fitting burial for their fallen monarch, and interred his remains here at the Holy Trinity Church in Bosham. Eyewitnesses have said they have encountered a ghostly knight walking around the church. Could this be the ghost of King Harold, stomping around his final resting place?

IRON DUKE HOTEL, HOVE, EAST SUSSEX

In today's modern era of conglomerate companies and franchises it is difficult to come across independently run public houses, bars and taverns where the corporate appearance takes a back seat for some good old-fashioned high-level customer service in historic surroundings. Come to the Iron Duke Hotel on Waterloo Street in Hove and you will find just such a place.

The hotel was built in 1828 and was formerly the area's civic centre controlling the development that was Hove and Brunswick town. Being an administration centre, such as it was, one can easily understand the importance of the building; 'it was allegedly the first place to be built around here and all the other buildings sprung up around it soon after,' said Peter Lindars, the Iron Duke's current landlord. 'We have a pretty good knowledge about the history of the hotel as a previous landlord, about ten years ago, researched it all really well. The Iron Duke has also been known as the Kerrison Arms and the Hove Lawns Hotel; it's rumored to have a tunnel that was constructed by smugglers that runs from the pub to the seafront, which is only a hundred or so yards away so it's perfectly plausible even though it's never been proven for sure.'

So, with a well-researched, checkable history in place it should be easy to discover who the ghosts and ghouls that haunt the Duke are and why they remain. Not so. The hotel has a collection of spooks within its walls but, as Peter told me, 'they all seem to be recurrent ones'. When I asked Peter what he meant about this he told me about a group that had recently conducted a paranormal investigation at the site and whose medium had picked up on a variety of ghosts but they seemed to wander throughout the building. For example, Mr Lindars told me, 'the medium picked up on a man in the bar area who is there with a dog, but there is also a man in the upper parts of the building and he has a dog as well. The ghost of a lady has been witnessed in room two by a medium and also by a gentleman who was staying in the room. Right above room two we have room five and a man there woke up one night with a ghostly woman sitting on the end of his bed and I often think it's the same ghosts just wandering around really.'

The cellar also seems to be a place of interest. Any type of room or area that is enclosed and usually darker than normal surroundings will always breed a certain type of reluctance and psychological effect as to what may, or may not, be lurking in the darkness. The Iron Duke Hotel claims to have the spirit of what a medium described as 'an angry man'. The cellar also has two areas that one could well assume were former holding cells from the time when the hotel was used as a magistrate's court . . . talk about a multi-purpose building!

A former cleaner at the hotel claims to have witnessed the ghost of a female child on the 'back staircase and a medium also picked up on the ghost of a girl in the cellar' said Peter. Why do these ghosts linger? Is it for the comfort of the hotel? The welcoming and happy disposition of the landlord? Or perhaps they stay here for some other reason. In 1907 the hotel suffered a serious fire that 'absolutely gutted the place'. Perhaps the ghostly occupants of the Iron Duke are victims from this tragic accident or maybe even past owners just keeping an eye on what's happening in their former home.

If you would like to experience one of the hotel's ghosts then Peter and his staff would be more than happy to hear from you. Book yourself into room two or five and do let me know if you experience anything untoward!

Iron Duke Hotel
3 Waterloo Street
Hove
East Sussex
BN3 1AQ

www.irondukebrighton.co.uk

KING AND QUEEN PUBLIC HOUSE, BRIGHTON, EAST SUSSEX

Tim Brown, one of the founders of the Paranormal Investigation Group Sussex, stumbled on the hauntings at the King and Queen Public House in Marlborough Place, Brighton, after a friend of his, who works at the pub, alerted him to the supernatural occurrences that were going on at the place. 'Staff members had reported hearing footsteps in a hallway even though there was no one there, feelings of sudden and inexplicable dread abound by the area of the ladies' toilet and one staff member even reported bearing witness to an apparition in the kitchen," said Tim. In August 2009 Tim and his team descended on the pub in the hope of explaining some of the more unusual occurrences that have been reported.

The King and Queen Public House in Brighton. Could the distressing conditions of a suicide and a murder victim be responsible for the ghosts that walk here? Photo © Matt Laker

The history of the pub looked interesting enough. The first building here was constructed in 1722 but the current building dates from the 1930s. The venue was first given a liquor license in 1729 in order to provide refreshments for sporting events that took place on the green. There was also historical evidence for some possible candidates who might actually be the ghosts haunting the pub. The first one dated from 1822, 100 years after the building was first constructed, and was one Thomas Blamey. Thomas was a soldier who was accused of stealing two shillings. Even though he protested his innocence, even in a letter to his father in which he wrote that he would 'sooner die than lose his character', Thomas felt that he simply could not deal with the shame of the accusation and decided to take his own life. The verdict of an inquest held in response to the suicide drew the conclusion that Mr Blamey was suffering from 'lunacy'.

Another potential candidate is John O'Dea. This gentleman and his friend, John Flood, were childhood friends and both enlisted into the Eighteenth Hussars. They were each other's equals both in life and rank but that did not stop John Flood extracting a most heinous punishment onto his life long friend for a minor misdemeanor. According to records, Mr O'Dea had not cleaned his friend's saddle to a sufficiently high enough degree and his friend threatened him with a disciplinary hearing; however, this never transpired and what exactly occurred between the friends is unknown. What is known though is that Private Flood shot his friend, killing him and possibly creating the ghost that now haunts the King and Queen. Private O'Dea was killed just inside the barracks' gates, which the present pub was expanded over during its rebuilding in 1931. Could these two tragic deaths present to us an explanation for the paranormal events that still occur in the King and Queen?

KINGLEY VALE, STOUGHTON, WEST SUSSEX

Kingley Vale is an area of outstanding natural beauty and special scientific interest due to the variety of flora and fauna present in the region.

Kingley Vale consists of over 500 acres of rural tranquillity and many visitors to the area come here to admire the amazing collection of yew trees that are estimated to be around 2,000 years old, making them the oldest living organisms in the United Kingdom. The vale has been known to mankind for thousands of years. Bow Hill, part of Kingley Vale, exhibits the remains of a long gone civilisation as this is where evidence can be found of Bronze Age burial mounds. It is in the region of these mounds that a local horse rider, Maria Preston, had a very strange encounter here back in the 1980s.

Ms Preston takes up the story: 'I was riding my horse, Elisa, who was a very forthright horse, not scared of anything, when all of sudden she froze and refused to move on,' Maria told me. Eager to discover why the horse could not be spurred on by her rider I asked Maria to explain if she knew of the reason as to why her horse would not proceed. 'Simple,' Maria replied. 'I looked over and hovering there, in a bush, was this white clad, transparent, female figure. She had a tiny face, some kind of monastic cowl over her head which made me think that the woman was some kind of druid, and she had her hands pressed together as if she was praying.'

Did the spectral figure realise that it had spooked horse and rider? 'No. The ghost, because that's what it was plain and simple, didn't notice we were there. Eventually I managed to push my horse on and off we went. I had my friend with me when this occurred and both of us saw the same ghostly woman. After we rode off we were so shaken by what we had just witnessed that we decided to return home, the only way home that we knew of meant going past the ghost again. As we approached the area of where we saw the woman we rode our horses rather quickly past. We didn't fancy seeing her again!'

With Kingley Vale being an area popular with walkers, ramblers, horse riders and nature enthusiasts I wonder if this phantom woman has been witnessed by other people using the area. If so then I would be very interested in hearing from you and I can be contacted via The Hampshire Ghost Club: www.hampshireghostclub.net.

KINGS HEAD PUBLIC HOUSE, CUCKFIELD, WEST SUSSEX

When I initially started to research the unusual world of ghouls, ghosts, spooks and spectres, one of the first ghost stories that I came into contact with was the story of Geranium Jane.

Jane was a servant working at the Kings Head and had become involved with the landlord in an illicit love affair. When Jane announced she had fallen pregnant with the landlord's child he decided that some action must be taken against Jane to prevent the news from becoming public knowledge.

When Jane was working one day the landlord launched a pot geraniums from an upstairs window, promptly striking Jane and killing her, hence how she got her name . . . Geranium Jane!

Although Jane has been very quiet in her appearances for some years now, there is a small collection of people who state they have witnessed the ghost of Jane. She apparently takes a liking to men staying at the Kings Head who are having extra marital rendezvous and makes her presence known to these men by causing a sharp drop in temperature in their bedrooms and shaking their beds violently. At least three children also claim to have seen her. Two children, who were playing in the upstairs rooms of the Kings Head, saw a woman with make-up streaming down her face who was not a member of the land of the living, and another child witnessed a pair of ghostly hands flying around the bar area.

KNEEP CASTLE, WEST GRINSTEAD, WEST SUSSEX

Kneep Castle has a history that stretches back to the time of the great Battle of Hastings in 1066 when William, Duke of Normandy, invaded the shores of merry old England in his successful attempt to seize the English crown.

Kneep Castle established itself, over successive generations, as a very popular deer park and was frequented by the likes of King John, Henry III, Edward II and Richard II. The herds of deer at Kneep appear to have been such an important aspect of the castle that the ghost that still haunts its grounds is indeed said to be able to transfigure herself into that of a deer; when not in her animal form the apparition is said to take on the image of a thirteenth-century girl. Who the mysterious shape shifting girl is and why she remains at Kneep is a complete mystery!

LION HOTEL, NYETIMBER, WEST SUSSEX

The county of Sussex has been fairly well used by the smuggling fraternity over the years and during my journey, researching and investigating the hauntings of this county, it became quite common to come across stories related to smuggling, either directly, or somewhat indirectly at times. The Lion Hotel is no different. This fifteenth-century building harbours the ghost of a mistress to one of the smugglers that used to frequent the place. It's claimed she was killed as she knew more than she should in regards to the smugglers' illegal operations. The ghost mainly frequents the ground floors and is known to walk through Room 5 and into Room 6. Although she has been witnessed at times, hearings seem more frequent than sightings of her. If you should be staying at this hotel then be on your guard for the sound of the ghost's swishing dress.

MEETING HOUSE, MEETING HOUSE LANE, BRIGHTON, EAST SUSSEX

The meeting house in Meeting House Lane has been privy to the sound of ghostly footsteps over the years, but the most interesting haunting originates not from actually within the meeting house itself, but outside in Meeting House Lane.

During the Second World War a female firewatcher witnessed the apparition of a grey hooded figure, now known as the Grey Nun, make her way down Meeting House Lane. The firewatcher apparently called out to the spectre but got no reply. Perhaps she didn't actually realise what it was she was witnessing, but that must have changed when she saw the ghostly figure disappear into the meeting house through an old, bricked up doorway!

MERMAID INN, RYE, EAST SUSSEX

Anyone who has an interest in ghosts and the paranormal, no matter how small or passing, would have undoubtedly heard about the hauntings at the Mermaid Inn in Rye.

This amazing inn has its roots way back to 1156, although it proudly boasts that it was rebuilt in 1420 after having been burnt to the ground by a marauding French fleet in 1337. As a result of the high reputation that the inn has acquired over the years, it comes as no surprise to find that not only does your normal everyday person use the inn, but that it has also been frequented by some very famous people including Charlie Chaplin, the Queen Mother, King George I and even the stage and screen superstar, Johnny Depp.

Having such a rich history means that the Mermaid Inn has not only been used by the friendly and famous but has also been used by the deadly and infamous. The inn was a well known frequenting spot of the notorious Hawkhurst Gang. This gang of smugglers, who were active from 1735 to 1749, robbed and killed from the borders of Dorset right through to regions of Kent and were eventually stopped following the executions of the gang's leaders, Arthur Gray and Thomas Kingsmill, in 1748 and 1749 respectively. There has, to date, been one report from a passerby who claims to have seen the ghosts of some of the members of the Hawkhurst Gang sitting in the Mermaid Inn with their pistols on the table. This story has never been confirmed and there have been no further occurrences of these spectres so personally I treat this account very lightly indeed. The gang is also linked to the ghost of a woman who haunts the inn. It is said that the young lady was romantically involved with one of the smugglers but his friends became somewhat wary that she could let vital and incriminating information slip out. They decided they could not take the risk and murdered the poor, unfortunate girl. Perhaps it's her wraith who has been seen in Room 5 or perhaps it's her ghost that haunts Room 1, sitting in a rocking chair in the corner and making the sleeping guests clothes dripping wet!

Room 18 is the haunt of a portly gentleman who takes to sitting on the ends of people's beds. But the most interesting story in recent years comes from Room 10 when a guest was staying overnight here with his wife. The couple witnessed the phantom form of a man emerge from a wall and make its way across the room and then disappear right through the opposite wall. The couple was so shaken by their experience that they decided to spend the rest of the night in the inn's downstairs lounge and even refused to return to their room to collect their luggage.

The inn is famous for its ghostly duelers. Room 16 has been the scene, on several occasions, where occupants of the room have awoken in the middle of the night to find a phantom fight being performed in front of their very eyes. The two duelers, two men dressed in doublet and hose and each carrying rapiers, struggle to the death until one of them is run through and falls to the floor. The surviving combatant then drags his vanquished foe to the corner of the room and disposes of the body down a now sealed up oubliette. The ghostly warriors have mostly been seen around 29 October and although they don't appear every year it is worth booking Room 16 around this time just to see if you could be the next eyewitness of these two fighters locked in mortal combat for all eternity!

Apart from people actually seeing the ghosts at the Mermaid Inn, other reported supernatural events include dragging sounds, whispering, objects being moved, a rocking chair moving to and fro on its own volition, footsteps and the sounds of clashing metal.

MICHELHAM PRIORY, UPPER DICKER, EAST SUSSEX

Back in 2002 a revolutionary new type of television programme hit our TV screens. That phenomenon is known to many as *Most Haunted*, a programme I have worked on, albeit for a short period.

The show, love it or hate it, as the show has a vastly divided viewing audience, started its run with a pilot being filmed at Michelham Priory. Michelham Priory has been known to paranormal investigators for years as a place that harbours supernatural secrets but *Most Haunted* can be credited with truly putting the place on the map and bringing the priory to the attention of many newcomers to the world of paranormal investigation.

Michelham Priory has many haunting tales to tell and is a place well worthy of intense investigation.

The priory was built in 1229 to house the religious order of the Augustinian Canons. Here they worshipped and lived until the dissolution of the monasteries under King Henry VIII, when their priory was taken away from them in 1537 and subsequently turned into a home with the most notable family owning the property being the Sackvilles.

It's not surprising to find ghosts here and, what with the priory being a former religious house, its collection of spooks and phantoms would, of course, not be complete without the ghost of your obligatory monk (or in this case one of the Augustinians Canons). This ghost has been seen in the area of the gatehouse and it has often been thought to be the apparition of John Leem, a very business-savvy prior who controlled the priory from 1374 to 1417. Back in 2004 I had the privilege of investigating Michelham Priory. When I and the team from the Hampshire Ghost Club arrived at the site we busied ourselves with setting up the equipment we would use during the course of the night, and whilst we were in and out of the building I had a very unusual encounter. I came through the undercroft and entered the main entrance of the building upon which I was confronted by the ghost of a brown-clad monk standing at the base of the staircase. The monk raised his hand and using his index figure on his right hand pointed upstairs and

The prior's room at Michelham Priory.

then proceeded to shout in a very loud voice 'He is a fucking sick bastard' and then promptly vanished. Unfortunately I was on my own at the time due to the investigation not starting. A member of the team entered seconds after the ghost had vanished and I asked them if they had heard the man shouting. Their reply was 'No. I ain't heard or seen anything yet.'

Another ghost that has been reported a number of times is that of a sad looking woman who is seen staring into the moat that surrounds Michelham Priory. The woman is commonly thought to be a member of the Children family who were tenants here for some years and allegedly lost one of their sons when his clothing became tangled in the watermill mechanism and strangled him to death. Although the graves of young members of the Children family can be found in Arlington Church, the story of the boy's death remains unconfirmed.

As I said, back in 2004 I was lucky enough to investigate the priory and our contact at the priory was Chris Tuckett, the property manager. Chris was very much a sceptical gentleman when he first moved into the priory but this changed quite quickly. He told us that shortly after moving in he awoke in the night to the sound of moving furniture. Chris is a very straight-thinking gentleman and not soft in his personality so I was quite shocked when he told me that when he heard the sounds he hid under the bedclothes. After a while, and plucking up courage, he ventured out in order to discover what it was he had heard. Chris noticed that a a piece of furniture had moved slightly and was somewhat surprised that the amount of noise he had heard was not representative of the amount of movement the piece of furniture had exhibited. He then noticed that one of the casters that the furniture had stood on was totally seized up with the varnish that it had scraped off the wooden floorboards whilst being moved; it was then he noticed a large figure of eight pattern that had been scratched onto the floor, scratches that could only have been made by the furniture being moved repeatedly in the same fashion.

Mr Tuckett also described to me how one evening, soon after moving in, he came in to the priory and started to make his way upstairs and met a man coming down the staircase. Thinking nothing of it and thinking the man was possibly another resident he ignored the gentleman. After getting further up the stairs Chris remembered he had locked the priory up and there was no way the gentleman on the stairs, whom he had passed, would be able to get out. Chris made his way back down the stairs in order to let the man out but was somewhat shocked to find that there was no one else in the building and what's more . . . there was no way the man could have left the building. Chris had locked up and had the only set of keys still on his person!

MINT HOUSE, PEVENSEY, EAST SUSSEX

Opposite Pevensey Castle lies Mint House. The current house that stands to this day was constructed in 1342 and is the site of a most horrific murder scene. Thomas Dight rented the house in 1586 with his mistress, but Thomas was in for a shock when he returned home early one night and found his mistress in bed with another man. Outraged at the betrayal, Thomas took his revenge. He tied his mistress up tightly and then proceeded to cut out her tongue, leaving her to bleed to death, but not before she had the time to watch her lover being roasted alive over an open fire. With such an awful way to die is it any wonder that the ghost of this woman has been reported on numerous occasions? One eyewitness even claims to have seen the woman's face pressed against a window before she passed through the solid wall. Even to this day there are some that claim they have seen the sad expression of the slaughtered woman looking out through the windows of Mint House.

MOTHERCARE SHOP, CHICHESTER, WEST SUSSEX

Can you imagine how the future will look? Can you imagine the wonder that children of the past would show playing with the modern-day toys that we have in this era? Well, in Mothercare, children from the past have just this privilege. Chichester is a very historic city and its connections to the Romans are for ever entwined in the fabric of its history. Being an old Roman city it's no wonder to discover Roman remains are literally ten a penny and many of the modern-day buildings that we now shop in are actually built upon Roman remains, cemeteries being a particular favourite. Could it be that the Mothercare store stands upon one of these resting places for the dead? Perhaps that would explain why staff at the store have claimed to have seen ghostly children and heard their laughter. What fun these children of the past must be having with the toys of today!

NAN TUCK'S LANE, BUXTED, EAST SUSSEX

Here we have a little mystery in the form of a legend that has two different endings and two slightly different characters.

In the civil parish of Buxted lies a lane known as Nan Tucks. The lane was named after the demise of a villager who was hounded by the community and their hate campaign against her led to poor Nan Tuck taking her own life. There are two slightly different versions of this story and both say the following events occurred in the seventeenth century, so I relate them both now.

Version 1. Nan Tuck was a young lady who was not the brightest of village folk; some say that she had mental illness which was the cause of her strange looks and simpleton personality. After a while the villagers started to blame problems that had affected the village on Nan Tuck and opinion soon mounted against her. The villagers were sure she was a witch and therefore must be dealt with in the tried and tested fashion of a ducking stool. The villagers roused an angry mob and chased after Nan. Nan fled to the local church and asked for help from the parish vicar but he turned the poor helpless lass away. Fearing for her life she fled down the lane that has now become known to us as Nan Tuck's Lane. After a while the villagers broke their pursuit of Nan and returned home. The following day the young lady's body was found swinging from a branch in Tuck's Wood. The raging mob had caused Nan to take her own life through the fear of what may lie ahead for her!

Version 2. Nan Tuck was an old lady and as the ravages of time took hold of the senior citizen the villagers thought that she was looking more and more like a witch so must be one. They decided to get the witch before the witch got them basically and, as per version 1 of this legend, chased the old lady down a lane which is now known as, yep, you guessed it, Nan Tuck's Lane. This story though ends slightly different with some sources saying the lady escaped and was never seen again and some saying that the old lady's body was found swinging from a branch in Tucks Wood.

Whatever the true story concerning the demise of Nan Tuck, or indeed even how old she was, what cannot be denied is that people have had some strange encounters on Nan Tucks Lane, and reports of a 'dark grey figure gliding and flitting along' have even been reported by people who know nothing of the story. One famous witness to the apparition was paranormal investigator and author Andrew Green. His account of his experience is relayed in his 1977 book, *Phantom Ladies*, and I quote, 'It was one evening in 1971, at a time when I had no knowledge of this story, that I was driving along the lane and was puzzled by a shadow which persistently kept just in front of my headlights moving in the hedgerow. Risking blocking the twisting road, I stopped to check my lights. There was no cause for the peculiar impression so I resumed my journey, but for at least half a mile this human sized and shaped darkness kept flitting along. Then suddenly, it was not there any longer.'

Did Mr Green encounter the ghost of Nan Tuck? If so, was the ghost fleeing from Mr Green's car with the thought that her pursuers had once again resumed their hunt?

OLD POLICE CELLS MUSEUM, BRIGHTON TOWN HALL, BRIGHTON, EAST SUSSEX

Back in June 2007 I was fortunate enough to be asked to attend and participate in an investigation of the Old Police Cells Museum that lies underneath the Brighton town hall.

Just after arriving at the museum, my wife, who attended this investigation and many more with me, decided that she needed to freshen up before the investigation started and was quite surprised when the lavatory door lock started to unlock itself and the door started to be forced open; opening the door quickly, intending to discover who was doing such a thing, proved a little bit of a shock as there was no one there! Despite a thorough inspection of the area there could be no rational reason as to why this happened. Certainly no one living and in attendance with the rest of the team was responsible for event.

One of the main reasons for the investigation being called was that staff at the museum had reported unexplained movements of objects in the building. The object in question was a blanket. In cell number one there is a mannequin of a prisoner lying in the cell's bed and the staff often reported witnessing this blanket having been moved from its display position. Could it be the ghost of Chief Constable Solomon?

Henry Solomon was the chief constable of Brighton from 1838 until his untimely death on 14 March 1844. A gentleman by the name of John Lawrence, who was being interviewed after being caught for stealing a roll of carpet, grabbed a poker from the open fireplace and then struck Henry across the side of the head, causing a fatal injury. The blow was so severe it was said to have bent the poker. The whole sordid affair had been witnessed and Lawrence met justice at the of the hangman's noose.

I remember on that dry and warm June night that, although we didn't see the ghost of Chief Constable Solomon, or any ghost for that matter, we were privy to some unusual occurrences that we could not explain. Footsteps coming from the floors above us even though we were the only ones in the building, flitting humanoid shadows and sensations of being watched were some of the reported phenomena. One of the most interesting pieces of 'evidence' on the night, though, was the sound of a girl's voice saying 'Hello'. This certainly was not one of the team members. The unexplained voice had been captured on my camcorder and still defies rational explanation to this day.

Perhaps more haunts the Old Police Cells Museum in Brighton than just the poor, murdered soul that is Henry Solomon?

PASHLEY MANOR, TICEHURST, EAST SUSSEX

The sounds of banging doors and falling crockery have been reported at Pashley Manor, as has the appearance of a pair of phantom hands. There has also been at least one report of a full-bodied manifestation witnessed here, that was apparently solid above the waste, its legs being nothing more than a spectral mist. Despite my best attempts to discuss the hauntings with the current owners, they were somewhat reluctant to discuss any recent supernatural events at Pashley Manor. I guess we will have to remain in the dark as to whether anything paranormal has been experienced here in recent years.

PEVENSEY CASTLE, PEVENSEY, EAST SUSSEX

This fortification is a well known tourist attraction in the county. Built by the Romans in the fourth century, its history spans many generations but it is today more remembered as being the landing site of the invading Norman armies that arrived on the British shores under Duke William of Normandy in 1066. Although there are reports of a phantom Roman centurion patrolling the battlements, a ghostly monk and even a supernatural drummer boy still beating on his drum, the most interesting ghost that haunts here is that of a woman. A ghost that has two possible identities!

The remains of the Roman castle at Pevensey. Photo © Wikipedia by Piotr Zarobkiewicz.

The first candidate is Lady Joan Pelham. Joan was the wife of Sir John Pelham who was the constable of Pevensey Castle from 1394. The Pelhams were supporters of Henry IV and when the monarch called upon his friend for his assistance in battling against Richard II they immediately responded. Sir John left for Yorkshire in order to engage Richard II's troops but, whilst he was away, a Yorkist army laid siege to Pevensey Castle. Although Sir John and his army were away, his wife, Lady Joan, held out valiantly against the attackers and even managed to get word to her husband on what was happening at home. It wasn't long before Sir John returned to the castle with his forces and lifted the siege. It's said that the phantom form of a lady, who walks the walls of Pevensey Castle, is none other than Lady Joan. Then again, there is another possible identity to this apparition. Some believe the ghostly lady is Queen Joanna of Navarre who was the wife of Henry IV and the stepmother of Henry V. Queen and stepson got on very well together for some time but Henry V eventually made the claim that Queen Joanna was a witch, a serious accusation at the time that could lead to one's execution. What the motives were behind Henry's claims no one knows. Did he genuinely believe she was a witch? Did he want her out of the way so he could have her fortune? At the end of the day we cannot be sure what his motives were but what we do know is that after three years of imprisonment Henry had a change of heart and released his stepmother and restored her wealth and position. As a result of the imprisonment of the Queen here at Pevensey Castle some believe the ghost of the lady of the battlements is Queen Joanna.

PEVENSEY COURTHOUSE, PEVENSEY, EAST SUSSEX

Brian Lambert and Jan Cox, volunteers at the Pevensey Courthouse and Pevensey own Trust, were able to tell me some of the history of this surprising little building. 'The courthouse is a building you can quite easily miss but it's a real treasure with its history and the ghosts we have here. The current building dates from the 1500s and there is evidence to suggest that a previous building, constructed from wattle and daub, existed on the site and was also used a courthouse.' Brian is also a respected paranormal investigator in his own right and founder of the UK British Paranormal Association – www.ukbpa.org.

Looking at the size of the building it would be hard to imagine being confined within its cells for any long period of time. Brian told me though that this was not the court's function: 'It's not a custodial place it's a corporate place,' Brian said. 'This was the place where corporal punishment was handed out. There are not many surviving records of the punishments here that were issued but we do know that in the fourteenth century a lady named Mary Tyler was punished for stealing cloth. Her sentence was to be tied to the back of a horse and cart and then taken from Pevensey to Westham in Sussex. This is a distance of some 1 ½ miles there and then 1 ½ miles back again. For every full turn of the cart wheel Mary was whipped. There are no surviving records telling us what became of Mary. We don't even know if she survived such a nasty punishment.

'We also have a record concerning a well-to-do gentleman who was arrested for stealing. As a result of his social status and the stigma that came with being hanged, his crime was reduced to a lesser account of theft and he was ultimately sentenced to have his feet and hands bound and then thrown into the river to drown. That was considered more fitting to his social standing than a plain, simple hanging.'

Pevensey courthouse is already looking like a place that could be brimming with paranormal activity when one considers how much pain, emotional as well as physical, criminals from times gone by had to endure in order to repay their debt to society. 'Sometimes you walk in here and the atmosphere hits you in the face, other times it can be quiet. Activity here always seems to increase following the summer months,' concluded Brian.

Following hot on the heels of the history that Brian had told me about I was able to track down and speak to Clint Symonds who is the director of the Sussex Paranormal Research Group. Clint and his team have conducted a series of investigations into the courthouse and the ghosts that haunt here. 'We believe we

The Pevensey Courthouse in East Sussex. Investigations at this historic building have revealed some interesting spectres of times gone by. Photo © Brian Lambert

have come across at least three ghosts here. One is a small boy called William who is aged about six or seven years old. Then there's Ellie May, again about six or seven years old and finally there's the ghost of a former jailer who appears to still patrol the old courthouse and has been described as being accompanied by a strong smell of rum. He has also taken a liking to breathing down people's necks.

'The courthouse is pretty small,' continued Clint, 'so you get to know the place quite quickly and you get adjusted to the natural creaks and groans an old place like the courthouse makes. This means that when something unusual does occur you can react on that pretty quickly.' So what phenomena have Clint and the team from the Sussex Paranormal Research Group experienced during their hunts for the dead? 'One of the strangest things we have had is a weight scale move on its own; it also started to show signs of increased electromagnetic fluctuations surrounding it which we couldn't explain at the time and have not been able to do since. One of the strangest of things is the smell of burning rope and the sound of creaking ropes. There are two beams in the courthouse from which people were hanged and these timbers still have the burn marks in the wood where the ropes have moved to and fro under the strain of those perishing on the end.'

Pevensey Courthouse may be a small place but there is much history to discover here and what makes it better is that the courthouse is always interested in hosting ghost hunts for interested, like-minded individuals. So if you want to attend an organised ghost hunt or arrange a booking for a group you run yourself then why not drop the Pevensey Courthouse an email via their website: www. pevenseycourthouse.moonfruit.com. More information on Clint and the Sussex Paranormal Research Group can be found at www.sprg.co.uk.

PRESTON MANOR, BRIGHTON, EAST SUSSEX

Dating back to the early seventeenth century, Preston Manor has certainly increased its paranormal profile in recent years as numerous people who have investigated the manor claim to have had some unusual and extraordinary encounters. Preston Manor shot to fame in 2006 when it appeared in the highly popular Living TV series, *Most Haunted*.

The ghost of a medieval nun, who has come to be known as Sister Agnes, has been reported over the years, but what would a medieval nun be doing haunting a place built in around 1600? Well Adrien Joly, who is in charge of the historical interpretation of Preston Manor, was able to throw some light onto this little mystery. 'The building is much older [than the seventeenth century], and there has been a house on or near the site of the existing house at least since the Norman Conquest.' That would explain the ghostly nun who predates the manor's construction.

The drawing room of Preston Manor, Brighton. The site of ghostly encounters, doors locking on their own and numerous unexplained noises. Photo © Stuart Cox/Paranormal Tours

Despite falling into the public eye with its haunting in recent years, it seems that the ghosts at Preston Manor have been experienced for quite some time and the Stanford family, who owned the manor in the eighteenth century, had quite a few of their own encounters at the house. Adrien Joly was of great help to me in my quest in searching out the ghosts of Preston Manor and it seems that the Stanford family reported their encounters in letters written to their friends and family. 'She came straight to her, as if to speak,' one of the family's letters reports, as Lily MacDonald recounted her first encounter with a phantom lady whilst in the drawing room of the manor. Lily's sister, Diana, also claims to have seen the ghostly woman and wrongly thought it was one of the housemaids.

A visitor to the house, a level-headed and sceptical colonel, also witnessed the ghost and even spoke to it. 'Would you be so kind as to tell me who you are and why you come?' he asked; the reply came back that she was a nun who had been wrongly excommunicated and was unable to rest until her remains were buried in a churchyard. Following on from the colonel's conversation with the deceased woman 'the family decided to have a séance and they contacted Ada Goodrich Freer who was a famous spiritualist medium that had charm, charisma and intelligence. She was known to have the ability of crystal vision, shell hearing, automatic writing and the Ouija board, but she also claimed to be a sensitive and was well known by the Society of Psychical Research until she fell in disgrace for the notorious Ballechin affair.'

Mrs Goodrich Freer's communication with the phantom woman is recorded as follows:

'Go away.'
'Are we disturbing the spirit.'
'Yes.'
'Who are the ladies who haunt the place.'
'Agnes and Caroline.'
'Caroline, nun from 1535, used to be a church hostel, which was used by pilgrims when they go to Canterbury.'

When Agnes was mentioned, Caroline replied 'curse her. She was excommunicated for serious misdeeds.'

Agnes reappeared; they asked how they could help her. The answer was 'prove me innocent'.

A third presence appeared, 'Friar Martin', responsible for the excommunication of Agnes; he found later that she was innocent.

Of course none of this alleged evidence has ever been confirmed in the historical record and many people who have analysed Mrs Goodrich Freer's work since her death have stated they have found evidence of fraudulent behaviour, which casts a major shadow of doubt on her work at Preston Manor.

Regardless of the alleged 'spirit contact', there have been a whole host of supernatural occurrences at the manor. In addition to the ghost of Sister Agnes there is a further ghostly woman who has been seen, doors have been opened and closed on their own, lights switch themselves off, doors lock on their own volition and a rather spooky dismembered hand has been seen floating by a four-poster bed in one of the manor's bedrooms.

QUEENS HEAD, ICKLESHAM, WINCHELSEA, EAST SUSSEX

This public house, in the Rother district of Sussex, was constructed in 1632. It commands fantastic views of the surrounding countryside and the pub itself gives

The remains of the curious, and haunted, ruin that is Racton.

one a real olde-world-type feeling with its atmosphere that is cast by a plethora of old-looking wooden beams and various nik-naks from times gone by.

But of course, we are not here for the views, food or ales, although they are all somewhat excellent, but for its ghost. This time we have a haunting where the ghost has been positively identified. In 1910 a gentleman by the name of John Gutsell became the landlord at the Queens Head. Strangely, some sources list Mr Gutsell's Christian name as George but I have it on good authority that his name was actually John: perhaps he liked to be called George and that is where the error had crept in over the years. Anyway, I digress. In 1919 Mr Gutsell died in the pub where he had spent the last nine years of his working life and it seems that the ghost who haunts here is none other than John himself. Eyewitnesses to his spectre claim they have seen John's ghost sitting in a chair wearing a shirt and waistcoat.

RACTON RUIN, NR FUNTINGTON, WEST SUSSEX

Racton Ruin has always been somewhat of a little mystery for no one seems to know what it was built for. There are many well educated theories but the true answer is that no one knows for sure.

The tower was originally built in 1772 and was designed by architect Harry Keane. It is thought the tower's original purpose was that of a summer house; standing at eighty foot high that would certainly have been some summer house!

A lady, who wishes to remain anonymous, who knows the area well, told me that for many years there had been rumors that the tower had been used for witchcraft and Satanic worshipping practices, although this has never been confirmed for definite. One thing is for sure, the place certainly does have a very sinister and eerie feeling to it, but that could just be attributed to the run-down and heavily vandalised appearance of the tower now.

Local legend states the area surrounding the tower is haunted by the ghost of a young girl, in her early to mid-twenties, who has been seen wandering the lanes leading up to Racton Ruin. Who she is and why she chooses to haunt such an ominous place no one knows.

ROYAL HIPPODROME, EASTBOURNE, EAST SUSSEX

The Royal Hippodrome Theatre at Eastbourne, originally called the New Theatre Royal and Opera House, is one of a series of theatres in this large sprawling town that has been the home to many famous characters and personalities including Charles Dickens, Lewis Carroll and Sir Ernest Shackleton.

The theatre opened in 1883 and was designed by the famous theatre architect Charles John Phipps (1835-1897) and even though the theatre has been, and in many cases still is, considered to be in an unpopular area of the town, it has drawn such eminent actors, actresses, singers and performers as the likes of Norman Wisdom, Charlie Chaplin and Max Miller to name just a few. The theatre also appears to house a ghost, but not the ghost of a past performer who has failed to take his last curtain call, as one would assume, but that of a former stage manager who fell to his death.

I know from my own personal experiences in investigating the paranormal that theatres can be one of the most productive places for experiencing the weird and wonderful and I was very fortunate to be able to interview Clint Symonds, who investigated the theatre for the first time in 2008. Clint ranks the theatre as one of his all-time-favourite investigations and it's easy to see why from the experiences he reported during his time here in the dead of the night. 'As soon as you walk into the Royal Hippodrome you can feel the energy, you really do feel like you're being watched. We had quite a lot going on during our investigation that we simply could not explain no matter how much of a logical and rational approach we took. Footsteps, doors slamming, a very strange vibrating floor that seemed to come and go, a mysterious scraping sound on the walls and the rather disturbing sound of cackling laughter.'

If it is true that the only ghost that haunts here is of the former stage manager then it seems quite apparent that he is not shy about giving ghost hunters what

The Royal Hippodrome Theatre in Eastbourne. The hauntings at this popular theatre gave Clint Symonds and his investigation team an unforgettable 'amazing night of phenomena'. Photo © Sussex Paranormal Research Group

they want and readily produces phenomena for them. Mr Symonds has every intention of returning to the Royal Hippodrome to conduct further research and investigations and hopes for yet another 'amazing night of phenomena'.

SAINT MARY THE VIRGIN CHURCH, WESTHAM, PEVENSEY, EAST SUSSEX

This church is haunted by a phantom that is rarely seen but has been heard on frequent occasions, knocking on the door to the church. It is commonly thought that this is the ghost of a long-gone smuggler, who raps the door to ensure the coast is clear so he can move his illegal wares. People inside the church have opened the door in answer to the knocking only to find no one there. There is also the ghost of an old man who walks up and down the path from the church door to the gate. In the past, when he has been witnessed, people often mistake him for a member of the land of the living. Could it be that the knocking on the church door is not the smuggler at all? Could it be the old man banging on the entrance trying to gain access to the church but when no one answers his visitation he decides to leave the way in which he came . . . down the church path? If this is the case then why would he choose to vanish on the occasions when the knocks have been answered? One ghost or two at the church of Saint Mary the Virgin? You decide.

SAINT NICHOLAS' CHURCH, ARUNDEL, WEST SUSSEX

The church of Saint Nicholas is quite unusual as churches go, because this house of God is actually split into two: the result of a disagreement between the Catholic Duke of Norfolk and the Church of England vicar, the Reverend Arbuthnot. To this day half of this religious house is dedicated to Catholic services with the other end being dedicated to services for those of the Church of England persuasion.

The reason Saint Nicholas is famous in the annals of paranormal history is due to a rather unusual photograph that was taken by a visitor to the church in the 1940s. The visitor took a snap of the altar and when his processed photographs were developed he was presented with what appears to be the spectre of a man kneeling at the altar.

There have been many suggestions put forward to explain the ghostly picture, from a double exposure to the ghost actually being a woman who was cleaning the altar at the time the photo was taken, the lady being accidently missed by the photographer.

The true answer to the questions raised over the explanation for the strange image is that we shall never know the real answer. Was this a ghost caught on film, a member of the church staff or a camera malfunction? Something that may be added at this point, and possibly increases the chances of this photo being paranormal in origin, stems from the claim of an old church warden who stated that he had witnessed a spectral lady dressed in blue, with long white hair, knelt at the altar in apparent prayer.

SEA LIFE CENTRE, BRIGHTON, EAST SUSSEX

For many years now the aquarium on Brighton sea front has had a reputation for having the occasional spooky or unexplained thing happen; what probably doesn't help is the nearby sign stating 'Don't worry if you feel a slight chill. Many staff over the decades have reported strange and ghostly occurrences.'

The aquarium was opened in 1872 and was designed by the famed architect, Eugenius Birch (1818-1884), who was also responsible for the design of Brighton's famous West Pier, Eastbourne Pier and Hastings Pier, amongst many other accomplishments. The aquarium was an instant success amongst the swanky Victorian upper classes of the time, but after a few years its popularity declined and the property became used as an establishment for all types of entertainment including time spent as a museum and even as a cinema!

The aquarium today is what it was built to be: an aquarium. This popular tourist spot, which houses over 150 species of aquatic life incorporated into 57 displays, is now owned and operated by the successful Sea Life Centre chain. In order to get the most up-to-date information on a venue's hauntings and its ghosts, obviously the best place to go for the reliable, first-hand information required is directly to the source. I contacted the centre's manager, Max Leviston, to discover more about the aquarium's haunting!

With stories of strange lights, objects mysteriously moving on their own, electrical equipment being switched off with no apparent reason and at least one reported account of disembodied laughing, could it be that the aquarium was a hotbed of supernatural activity? That's what I thought at least.

Despite the above events being noted by various people throughout the years, it seems that Max was not able to help in my search for the ghosts of Brighton Sea Life Centre; he told me: 'If there are haunting tales surrounding the Sea Life Centre in Brighton then you will be enlightening us, as we are not aware of any!'

So if even the manager is not aware of any ghosts at the aquarium could it be that the previous reported supernatural occurrences are nothing more than one-off random events, naturally occurring mysteries that have somehow been embellished over the years and gathered momentum in a Chinese whispers sort of way, or could it be that there is actually more to the aquarium than even the manager knows at this present time?

SEVEN STARS, ROBERTSBRIDGE, EAST SUSSEX

'The Seven Stars is one of the top ten most haunted pubs in the country,' I was told by Caroline Boyde, who is the current landlady of this historic pub. The pub can trace its origins back to the twelfth century but the pub these day is a bit of a mix and match from different periods of history with the oldest parts dating back to around 1460.

Caroline has not been the landlady for long but she clearly demonstrates a passion towards her tavern in both its history and its paranormal occurrences. The Seven Stars is haunted by a ghost that is referred to as the red monk after a phantom cloaked figure, dressed in red, has been witnessed here. Many people with an interest in history will be aware that monks from different religious orders wore different colour habits: the Cistercians wore white, the Augustinians wore black, the Franciscans wore brown and so on and so on but what possible order could this spectral monk belong to or could it possibly not even be a monk at all?

The area around Robertsbridge has been entwined with some notorious people throughout its history and none more so than the infamous Hawkhurst Gang. This gang of smugglers and murderers plagued a vast area of land stretching from Poole in Dorset right through to the county of Kent. A famous incident occurred in Robertsbridge when the gang decided to raid a customs cart that was loaded with contraband tea: the gang were successful in their theft but left a customs officer, Thomas Carswell, lying dead. Could the phantom red monk in fact be the ghost of a former smuggler who once used the pub?

Caroline informed me that 'the red monk was last seen in 1972 and although he hasn't been witnessed since then we do get some very unusual activity occurring here, some of the regulars here have witnessed objects being thrown off the shelves. One of the strangest things that occurs here is the heating gets messed about with. I know for a fact at what level the heating is set for and I check it regularly and on quite a few occasions I have found the dial has been moved to a different setting and none of the staff here own up to changing the setting. I have also found strange footprints in the kitchen, which again, have no explanation.'

Despite being known as one of the most haunted pubs in England, Caroline told me that 'there are no bad feelings here whatsoever and I love the place'. Perhaps her love for the Seven Stars may prompt the ghost red monk to put in an appearance for Caroline sometime in the near future?

THE WINGROVE INN, ALFRISTON, EAST SUSSEX

The full history of the Wingrove Inn is going to be very well covered in a forthcoming book that has been written by Dr June Goodfield and Peter Robinson of the Alfriston and Cuckmere Valley Historical Association. June was able to tell me something of the history of this now somewhat swish and classy restaurant and hotel: 'The house was built by one Richard Porter in 1864 on loans and mortgage from a friend whom he never managed to pay off! Porter had been born in Dumfriesshire, had spent some time in London where he clearly got into the racing coterie and had a lively married life – having two wives, one older than him and one much younger – and no head for business! On his own admission, he made and lost at least three fortunes during his life.

'So the Wingrove itself was primarily the residence of a man who established racing stables in the village. For the next ninety-three years it remained just that – a private residence associated with a racing establishment. Sometimes the owner rented it out as a house and a racing stables, as did the infamous Horatio Bottomley who bought Wingrove from the man who had lent Porter the money. Bottomley never lived there but rented Wingrove to Batho for seventeen years until, in 1915, Batho moved out. However, five years later, in 1920, he finally bought Wingrove from the Bottomley creditors and associates and thus was both the owner of the house and the racing establishment. Unlike Bottomley, Batho was a highly successful trainer as well as a man of great integrity. Batho died in 1925; his widow sold the place to Baron Queensborough, and in 1930 a Frederick John Palmer Chapman joined him as a partner.'

One of the former owners of The Wingrove Inn, Susan Butcher, related some of her experiences to me whilst she worked at the venue: 'I am a rigorous sceptic but I too had strange experiences. A customer came to the bar saying someone was in the room he had booked into. I thought I had inadvertently double-booked the room so accompanied him upstairs to find no-one there.

'I certainly had some strange experiences at the hotel and I remember glasses used to frequently fly off the bar shelves and smash themselves on the floor. I was cleaning the bar carpet early one morning when about six jars of pickles and chutneys, prepared for that day's Sunday lunch, lifted from the table and upended themselves onto the floor, every one of them was in the same position. A man who looked after the building between landlords, said he often used to hear footsteps on the stairs and most frightening of all – particularly to my extremely practical husband – was the appearance of streaked numbers scrawled on a whitewashed wall behind the liquor store. They were not there one day, there the next. I even consulted the vicar about an exorcism but then we sold the business and retired. I often wondered whether the "spirit" survived the extensive refurbishment.'

VERDLEY CASTLE, NEAR MIDHURST, WEST SUSSEX

The thirteenth-century fortification that was Verdley Castle has long since vanished from the Sussex landscape, but there does remain one reminder of a time long ago. Verdley Castle was said to be the area where the last wild bear in the whole of England was slain; it was then eaten at a huge feast held for the local populace. It is said that the animal's spirit now wanders the area; some sources also say that the ghostly revellers also haunt the place. I have unfortunately been unable to track down a recent reliable sighting of the poor animal or the phantom party goers.

YE OLDE SMUGGLERS INN, ALFRISTON, EAST SUSSEX

Built in 1358 the Ye Olde Smugglers Inn has certainly had an interesting history and a variety of uses including that of a slaughterhouse and butchers. Probably one of the inn's most interesting and notorious characters in its colourful past comes from the inn's use as a butchers when the owner's son, Stanton Collins, took over the business from his father.

Stanton Collins was a well-known figure in the area for his associations with the Alfriston Smuggling Gang; for his crimes connected with these outlaws he was deported to Australia in 1830. The inn's first ghost could very well be associated with this time period, as landlord Cliff Nicholson, whose associations with the pub go back over thirty years, told me: 'There's two small cottages that were called number one and two slaughterhouse cottages; these were where the men who worked here lived. There's a passageway that runs between these cottages and the pub and the ghost of a woman wearing old-fashioned clothes has been seen. I have seen her, or at least what I considered to be a ghost of her. My dog used to react very strangely in the passageway at times, most of the time he was fine and then there were occasions where you could just not get him up there.'

The inn is spaced out on three levels and most of the ghostly occurrences appear to happen on the second floor of the building with no sightings or paranormal experiences being reported on the first floor. 'People have reported seeing the face of a ghost peering out of a window on the second floor; they usually see the apparition from the inn's beer garden.'

It's going well . . . two ghosts and counting . . . could there be more? 'The bar area is also interesting and we have had some patrons over the years that have said they have seen the ghost of an elderly man, wearing a flat cap and walking with a stick, and the ghost of a woman who appears to be associated with the man.'

GHOST HUNTING
– AN INTRODUCTION

One of the most common questions I get asked by people wanting to conduct their own ghost hunt is 'where do I begin?'

In this brief introduction I hope to cover some of the basics. Many would-be paranormal enthusiasts out there are under the impression that in order to investigate your own haunting you need lots of expensive equipment that can take years to acquire, and although this is true in order to conduct in-depth research, there are some basic items that will help you in your quest for the paranormal.

Your first step should be to compile an account of what has actually been occurring at your chosen haunted venue. Have there been sightings? Disembodied voices? Objects mysteriously moving around or sudden increases or decreases in temperature are all things that you would want to take into consideration. If a ghost has been spotted by someone at the property then try to get this witness account first hand; interview the person if possible as this will ultimately reveal the finer details of the encounter.

Once your background information on what has been experienced has been collected and organised you can then look into the history of the building and make notes of anything you consider that could be relevant to your investigation. Was there a tragic death on the premises? Was there a long period of occupation by a particular resident that could explain a ghost's reluctance to leave, could there be an emotional bond to the venue?

Ensure your background research is in-depth and as thorough as it can possibly be. All this information will help you at a later date and only when you have your dossier and a good working knowledge of your haunted location can your hunt begin.

When we discuss paranormal investigation equipment many people instantly rush into buying high-specification digital cameras or night-vision camcorders, but remember, one of the best pieces of equipment you can have is yourself, for you could be the next witness to the ghostly apparition you are investigating and your personal experience of the encounter will linger with you for years to come.

Equipment is obviously important, though, so ensure you purchase the best equipment you can in your price range and don't forget some very basic and essential items. Below is brief list of equipment that the beginning amateur ghost hunter will want to acquire.

- Pads and Pens
- Clipboard (very useful if a level surface cannot be found)
- Dictaphone (digital preferred)
- Digital camera (try to avoid cameras with a low megapixel rating)
- Camcorder and plenty of spare tapes or discs
- A torch and spare batteries

Pads and pens are important for recording essential information such as the times of experiences and also at what times certain experiments were established. Remember to take plenty of pens as they have the habit of running out at the most inconvenient times!

Clipboard. In many haunted places it is very common not to be able find a flat, level surface in order to make your notes or draw maps and diagrams; this is especially the case in haunted places such as graveyards and other external locations.

Dictaphones are essential if you choose to experiment with Electronic Voice Phenomena, or EVP for short. Many investigators have claimed that disembodied voices have been caught on a variety of recording devices and the dictaphone has now become an essential piece of any ghost hunter's kit. Recording EVP can range from being very simple to quite complex. As this guide is only a basic introduction I will explain the simple methodology for conducting your own EVP experiment. Once you are in your chosen location, and have a specific place in which you wish to do your recording, sit down quietly and start your dictaphone recording. At the start you should always state your name, the location, the time, persons present (get everyone to say their own name so you have a record of what their voice sounds like on the recording so it won't be mistaken for a ghostly voice later on) and also the weather conditions: stating the weather is very important as a ghostly moan on your recording may well be the sound of the wind outside if it is particularly windy. All you need to do next is to start asking questions. There is no minimum, or maximum, number of questions you should ask and the quantity is completely up to the individual ghost hunter but remember the quality of your questions is important. You should aim at asking specific questions so that any responses gauged can be checked and as a suggestion I would include some of the questions below:

- Can you tell me your name please?
- Did you live here?
- When did you live here?
- Can you make three knocks, taps, raps or bangs for me please?
- Can you tell me what today's date is please?

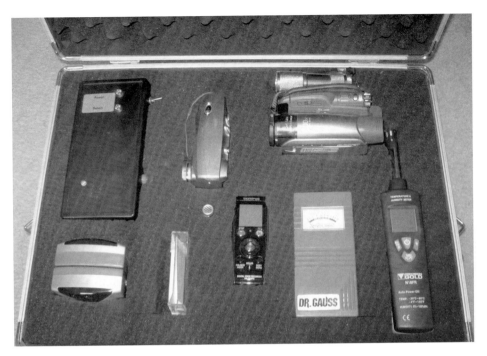

An example of some of the author's paranormal investigation equipment, all contained in a sturdy metal case which is an essential item in order to keep your equipment safe.

All of these questions could provide you with some interesting information and experiences should any possibly phantom voices be left in apparent response. Remember that after you ask each question leave a space before asking your next question so that any possible ghost that may be with you can give an answer to you. EVP is one of the most interesting and intriguing elements of paranormal investigation and is currently unexplained even though some very plausible and possible explanations have been offered, the jury is still out and the debate between supporters and opponents of EVP continues!

When using your digital camera it is always worth taking random photos and also asking for any ghosts that may be haunting the location to stand in front of the camera for you. I have tried this for over ten years, and although I have not had any luck with capturing that all-elusive ghost, your attempts might prove more successful. There are many anomalous photographs in the public domain these days and it's worth doing some in-depth research into causes and explanations for some of the most commonly caught phenomena, or what is thought to be phenomena but usually has a rational explanation.

If you're going to use a camcorder on your ghost hunt then try to set it at the widest angle so you cover as much of the area in question as possible; it is always best to have more than one camera filming an area. If you manage to capture an apparition on film then the image on two cameras is obviously better than on just one. In recent years night-vision camcorders have become very popular in the ghost hunting community but unless you're willing to spend in excess of £700 you may find your night-vision rather disappointing and will probably need an additional laminator for your camera to film better in low-level light conditions. Always use brand new tapes and never record over your old tapes even after you have transferred the film to your computer or other media.

A torch is always required as most people conduct their investigations at night. This is only done to limit the disturbance caused by passers-by and there is no reason at all why you can't ghost hunt in the daytime. In fact, some of my best results have been captured in the broad daylight hours.

I hope this brief guide, and it is by no means comprehensive, has given you some food for thought in conducting your own ghost hunt; but before you get stuck into investigating your own haunting I would like to offer some simple words of wisdom to bear in mind when dealing with the supernatural!

- Have fun and don't lose sight of why you are there.
- Always get permission to investigate a location. Trespassing is illegal and gives ghost hunters a bad name so please don't do it!
- Always leave the venue in the condition you found it and take all your rubbish away with you.
- Stay calm. Many people can become quite over-excited on a ghost hunt and lose their rational thought.
- Always remain objective and never jump to conclusions.
- Always take a mobile phone with you in case of emergencies and tell someone where you are going and when you expect to be back.

If you would like more information on ghost hunting or would like to attend a ghost hunt then please feel free to visit the website of the Hampshire Ghost Club at www.hampshireghostclub.net and we would be happy to put you in touch with a group in your area.

Happy Hunting !

David Scanlan

GET INVOLVED

If this book has whetted your appetite enough and you would like to get involved and do some ghost hunting yourself then I can whole-heartedly recommend the following Sussex-based paranormal investigation groups. I am sure they would be more than happy to hear from you:

COTC Paranormal Investigations – www.cotcpi.co.uk
Sussex Paranormal Research Group – www.sprg.co.uk
West Sussex Paranormal Investigations – www.wspi.co.uk
Paranormal Investigation Group Sussex – www.the-pigs.co.uk
Sussex Paranormal – www.sussexparanormal.co.uk
British Paranormal Association – www.ukbpa.org

BIBLIOGRAPHY

Collins English Dictionary (2006)

Brooks, John, *Good Ghost Guide* (1994)
Evans, Sian, *Ghosts – Mysterious Tales from the National Trust* (2006)
Green, Andrew, *Haunted Sussex Today* (1997)
Green, Andrew, *Our Haunted Kingdom* (1974)
Green, Andrew, *Phantom Ladies* (1977)
Karl, Jason, *Jason Karl's Great Ghost Hunt* (2005)
Lewis, Roy Harley, *Theatre Ghosts* (1988)
Middleton, Judy, *Ghosts of Sussex* (1988)
Murdie, Alan, *Haunted Brighton* (2007)
Scanlan, David, *Paranormal Hampshire* (2009)
Scanlan, David, *Paranormal Wiltshire* (2009)
Underwood, Peter, *A-Z of British Ghosts* (1992)
Underwood, Peter, *Nights in Haunted Houses* (1994)
Underwood, Peter, *Ghosts and How to See Them* (1993)
Waugh, Mary, *Smuggling in Kent & Sussex, 1700-1840* (1985)
Weedall, Arron, *Haunted Chichester and Beyond* (2008)
Willin, Melvyn, *Ghosts Caught on Film* (2007)

ABOUT THE AUTHOR

The author outside a haunted church

David Scanlan, author of *Paranormal Wiltshire*, has had an interest in the paranormal since the age of eleven when his sister started to experience poltergeist phenomena in a house she had moved to in the northern suburbs of Portsmouth, Hampshire.

In 2001, after years of researching and investigating paranormal phenomena, David decided to use his knowledge and experience and create a paranormal investigation group, The Hampshire Ghost Club, www.hampshireghostclub.net. The group gained in popularity very quickly and established itself as a major player in the field of ghost research and investigation, a reputation it still holds today!

The group investigates allegedly haunted venues all over the UK and has conducted studies at some of England's most haunted venues including Levens Hall in Cumbria, Beaulieu Abbey in Hampshire, Dudley Castle in the West Midlands, Chingle Hall in Lancashire and many other high-class locations that are notorious for their haunted heritage. David has also acted as a consultant to various organisations such as the Royal Navy, County Councils and a peer of the realm.

Members of the public have previously seen the author's work, and indeed the work of the Hampshire Ghost Club, in various publications, on radio networks and TV. David starred in the first one-hour special of Living TV's popular show *Most Haunted*, and also in their first-ever live ghost hunt that was broadcast across the United Kingdom.

David was born in Portsmouth, Hampshire, and currently resides near Southampton with his wife and three children.

ALSO BY THE AUTHOR

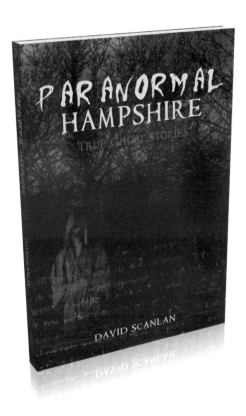

Paranormal Hampshire

Price: £12.99
ISBN: 978-1-84868-257-3

Available from all good bookshops or order direct from
our website www.amberleybooks.com

ALSO BY THE AUTHOR

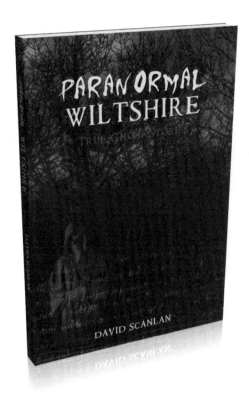

Paranormal Wiltshire

Price: £12.99
ISBN: 978-1-84868-461-4

Available from all good bookshops or order direct from
our website www.amberleybooks.com